Conflict Resolution Skills for Teens

D1567528

David Cowan
Susanna Palomares
Dianne Schilling

cover design by Nancy Clark

cover photo by William Bronston, MD

ISBN – 10: 1-56499-074-7

ISBN – 13: 978-1-56499-074-7

INNERCHOICE Publishing
15079 Oak Chase Court
Wellington, FL 33414

www.InnerchoicePublishing.com

Conflict Resolution
Skills for Teens

The strong man
is the man who can
stand up for his rights
and not hit back.

Dr. Martin Luther King, Jr.

Contents

    ES = Experience Sheet

Developing Conflict Resolution Skills 81

ES = Experience Sheet

Sharing Circles 115

HOW TO USE THIS BOOK

Conflict Resolution Skills for Teens is a developmental and sequential program of activities designed to 1) build a base of awareness, understanding, and skills required for conflict prevention and resolution, 2) give students practice using a variety of strategies for managing and resolving conflict, 3) create opportunities for students to apply those strategies to real-life problems and conflicts, and 4) encourage students to transfer their learning to the resolution of issues and conflicts in the family, community, nation, and world.

Conflict Resolution Skills for Teens can be used in a variety of settings. It is appropriate for classrooms, group counseling programs, adolescent treatment facilities, alternative school programs, camps, and leadership training efforts of all kinds. If you have a peer mediation program in your school, incorporate the activities into your existing mediator training workshops.

In order for the activities to have the impact intended, we strongly urge you to present the units in the order given. Many activities are built on a foundation of skills presented in earlier activities.

For optimum benefits, each section must be covered thoroughly. For example, implementing a negotiation or problem-solving activity (from "Developing Conflict Resolution Skills") before the students have been introduced to active listening (in "Fundamental Skills Related to Conflict Management") will prove less than fully effective. You don't have to implement every activity in each section, but do provide a sufficient number of experiences to ensure that the skills and concepts being taught receive plenty of practice and reinforcement.

Many of the activities in the units titled "Understanding the Nature of Conflict" and "Developing Conflict Resolution Skills," include a section of important information under the subheading, "Information to Share." This section summarizes some of the main concepts and discussion points upon which the activity is based. A thorough reading of this section will help prepare you to lead the activity. During the activity, refer back to the section from time to time to be certain that you have covered the key points.

Throughout the activities, you will see an occasional sentence or paragraph in italics. Most italicized sections are sample <u>scripts</u> — word-for-word presentations or questions that advance the course of the activity. You are not expected to use these scripted sections verbatim; they are models. Using your own words is almost always preferable. In addition, we encourage you to adjust and modify the language and demands of all activities to suit the ages, ability levels, cultural/ethnic backgrounds, and interests of your students. You will know best how to maximize the appropriateness and impact of each activity, so please take those liberties.

At the conclusion of every activity, you will encounter a list of discussion questions. Always try to allow enough time to facilitate a brief summary discussion. Students benefit most from an activity when they are given the opportunity to talk about the experience immediately afterwards, verbalizing their insights and making connections to events and conditions in their lives. Whenever possible, we urge you to solicit answers, solutions, questions, and examples from your students, making the activity highly relevant and personal.

Occasionally you may wish to build a bridge to issues the students are dealing with in the classroom, school, or community. To do so, substitute a discussion question of your own. However, do not use the summary discussion to sermonize or lecture, or to force connections that the students are not ready to make. Do keep the questions open-ended (requiring more than a "yes" or "no" response), attempt to stimulate higher-level thinking, and facilitate, facilitate, facilitate.

Our unique discussion process, the Sharing Circle, has been allocated a special section at the end of the book. Please don't segregate them in actual practice. When the students are working on a particular concept or set of skills, go through the circles (and the list of additional circle topics) and select a Sharing Circle that seems particularly relevant.

Sharing Circles are extremely valuable. They can generate a wealth of insights and help deepen the relevance of virtually any concept or subject. Unquestionably, repeated participation in circles is one of the most potent ways to develop awareness and learning in the realm of conflict resolution.

Introduction and Overview

Conflict, violence, and bullying are escalating in schools nationwide. Educators today express unprecedented concern about school and classroom disruptions that steal instructional hours and endanger the safety of students.

Some amount of conflict occurs normally in all schools. However, schools that are large, have limited resources, or serve highly diverse populations often experience pervasive conflict. Outside the school, a corresponding escalation in aggressive and violent behaviors exists in society at large. Our culture inadvertently supports violence through advertising, social relationships, politics, the media, and entertainment. At the same time, a serious and continual breakdown in the nuclear family often leaves the job of parenting to the nation's educators.

Often, conflicts escalate because students and the adults around them don't know how to respond to disagreements and confrontations pro-socially and creatively. Peers — sometimes even parents —reward aggressive responses to conflict. These responses are modeled on television and in movies, where even the "good guys" maim and kill in order to "win." Obviously, our society and our schools are in critical need of people with effective pro-social conflict resolution skills.

Traditional discipline procedures (expulsion, time-out rooms, suspensions, and scolding) teach students to depend on authority figures to resolve conflicts, and in the process obstruct student ethical development. Total reliance on authoritarian approaches is a serious mistake with potentially dire consequences.

To cope with the institutional problems created by conflict, and to help students and staff handle conflict better, school-based conflict resolution programs have emerged as valid and promising alternatives to adult dominance. There are now thousands of school-based conflict resolution programs in the nation. Students are learning to fight fair, listen to each other's viewpoints, discuss their differences, seek compromise, and solve mutual problems. It is recognized that *conflict management is an essential skill for a democratic society*.

Where they exist, school-based conflict resolution programs have produced impressive results:

- Teachers report fewer fights and more caring student behavior.
- Administrators notice improved attendance and a dramatic decline in the number of suspensions. They spend less time on disciplinary matters.
- Students, parents, and teachers change their attitudes toward conflict. Instead of viewing conflict as a problem to be avoided or a prelude to negative confrontation, they see it as a process which defines values and leads to growth.

By enabling students to mediate their own disputes, educators may be synthesizing the finest potential in the school—the creative, constructive dynamic inherent in conflict.

CONFLICT RESOLUTION SKILLS FOR TEENS teaches students how to mediate disputes and negotiate solutions. It develops the ability of students to regulate their own actions by giving them opportunities to make decisions regarding how to behave and then follow through on those decisions. The program creates an environment of acceptance and high expectations, where conflict is handled creatively and pro-socially. It reduces violence and drastically diminishes the need for outside intervention.

Lack of understanding between individuals and groups who are different with respect to such things as race, religion, appearance, life-style, cultural values, and physical or other disabilities is one of the oldest, most pervasive sources of conflict. Because most of the activities and Sharing Circles in *Conflict Resolution Skills for Teens* involve students in a continuing dialog — an exchange of experiences, opinions, and feelings — students build a sound base for effectively dealing with conflict situations that stem from these differences.

Conflict Resolution Skills for Teens teaches all of these skills using a varied methodology heavily weighted with experiential, cooperative learning strategies. The activities serve as building blocks in a coherent curriculum for developing the skills and strategies of conflict prevention, management and resolution.

An Overview of the Thematic Units

The activities in *Conflict Resolutions Skills for Teens* are organized to focus on critical ingredients necessary to prevent conflict and to successfully manage and resolve conflict when it occurs. The following is a summary of the main components of each unit.

Fundamental Skills Related to Conflict Management

Many potential conflicts can be avoided by communicating effectively. In addition, students who have learned to listen well and express themselves accurately are better able to deal effectively with conflict when it occurs. However, communicating in the stressful environment that usually accompanies conflict requires much greater skill than does normal communication. The communication activities in this section are designed to help students learn specific communication strategies that are crucial to creative and positive conflict resolution.

No conflict is ever resolved without at least one decision — often several. Decision making is absolutely fundamental to conflict resolution. The issues of problem solving and decision making are given particular attention in this section. Students are helped to understand the processes and influences that shape decision making and problem solving and receive repeated practice in both processes.

Understanding the Nature of Conflict

In order to develop healthy, confident attitudes toward conflict and conflict resolution, students need to examine its nature — what it is, how it is born, how it grows, and how it dies. They need to face their prejudices and fears about conflict and see conflict for what it is — a necessary and normal process that can have positive or negative results, depending on how it is handled.

The activities in this section help students define conflict, identify common sources of conflict, and become aware of vocabulary and body language that tend to escalate and de-escalate conflict. The students are helped to recognize that most people respond to most conflicts with the same learned patterns of behavior, and each student assesses and evaluates the effectiveness of his or her own conflict style. As an alternative to the use of *unconscious* conflict styles, the students consider the value of developing a repertoire of *conscious* conflict strategies. Finally, students learn to differentiate between assertive, aggressive, and passive behaviors and understand how these behaviors tend to affect the life cycle of a conflict.

Developing Conflict Resolution Skills

Students need to become acquainted with a range of conflict management strategies, discussing the relative pros and cons of each. In addition, they need many opportunities to practice conflict management strategies safely and enjoyably, so that they can internalize and refine their skills.

This section includes specific strategies that help students handle both unexpected and planned confrontations, resolve conflicts, cope with and reduce anger, manage the residual feelings that follow conflict, and openly receive and evaluate criticism.

In addition to the role plays and other practice techniques imbedded in the activities, several additional approaches to behavioral rehearsal are outlined, including role-play variations, and the use of reading, writing, and art assignments — all appropriate for secondary classrooms and counseling groups. Finally, a number of role-play starters are provided in the form of conflict scenarios typical of those encountered by young people.

Sharing Circles

The Sharing Circle is a unique small-group discussion process in which participants share their feelings, experiences, and insights in response to specific, assigned topics. Sharing Circles are loosely structured, and participants are expected to adhere to rules that promote the goals of the circle while assuring cooperation, effective communication, trust, and confidentiality.

Over forty years of using Sharing Circles with students and educators world wide has demonstrated the power of the Sharing Circle in contributing to the development of conflict resolution skills. Circles can noticeably accelerate the development and internalization of the conflict strategies introduced in this book. They are a key ingredient in bringing about the growth necessary for students to engage in the level of *self*-management required to effectively manage and resolve conflict.

This section contains over twenty fully developed Sharing Circles, along with all of the information you need to become a skilled circle facilitator. Please do not attempt to lead a circle until you have read this introductory material. Then use circles liberally, allowing their innumerable benefits to venerate every aspect of your conflict program.

Fundamental Skills Related to Conflict Management

Many potential conflicts can be avoided by communicating effectively. In addition, students who have learned to listen well and express themselves accurately are better able to deal effectively with conflict when it occurs. However, communicating in the stressful environment that usually accompanies conflict requires much greater skill than does normal communication. The communication activities in this section are designed to help students learn specific communication strategies that are crucial to creative and positive conflict resolution.

No conflict is ever resolved without at least one decision — often several. Decision making is absolutely fundamental to conflict resolution. The issues of problem solving and decision making are given particular attention in this section. Students are helped to understand the processes and influences that shape decision making and problem solving and receive repeated practice in both processes.

What Stops Good Communication

Role-Play and Discussion

Objectives:

The students will:
— demonstrate common ways of responding to another person that may block communication.
— describe how different ways of responding may affect a speaker.
— discuss what constitutes effective and ineffective communication.

Materials:

one copy of the experience sheet, "The Communication Stoppers," for each student; whiteboard, or chart paper and magic marker

Directions:

Write the following list on the board or chart paper for the students to see when they enter class:
- Interrupting
- Challenging/Accusing/Contradicting
- Dominating
- Judging
- Advising
- Interpreting
- Probing
- Criticizing/Name-calling/Put-downs

Begin the activity by asking the students to think of a heading or title for the list on the board. Write their suggestions down and discuss each one briefly. Add the suggested title, "Communication Stoppers," and ask the students if they can imagine how these behaviors might have the effect of hampering communication—or stopping it altogether.

Pass out the experience sheet, "The Communication Stoppers," to each student. Discuss each communication stopper with the students by using the elaborations below. To further facilitate this discussion use the discussion questions on the following page after talking about each communication stopper.

Interrupting

Discussion: Point out how frustrating it is to be interrupted, and how futile it is to continue a conversation when interruptions occur over and over. Interrupting is probably the most frequent way in which communication is stopped.

Advising

Discussion: By giving unsolicited advice, a person immediately assumes a position of superiority. Advice-giving says, "I know better than you do." Advice may also cause the speaker to feel powerless to control his or her own life.

Judging

Discussion: Judging retards communication even when the judgment is positive. Not only does the "judge" assume a superior position, his or her evaluations may so completely contradict the speaker's own feelings that a contest or argument ensues—or further communication seems pointless.

Interpreting

Discussion: Interpreting and analyzing say that the listener is unwilling to accept the speaker (or the speaker's statements) at face value. Not to mention that the interpretation is frequently wrong.

Dominating

Discussion: We all know how frustrating and annoying it is to be in a conversation with someone who always has something better and more interesting to say than we do. In addition, when one person dominates a conversation, others are forced to use another communication stopper, interrupting, just to get a word in.

Probing

Discussion: Probing tends to put the speaker on the defensive by asking him or her to justify or explain every statement. More importantly, questions may lead the speaker away from what she or he originally wanted to say. The questioner thus controls the conversation and its direction.

Challenging/Accusing/Contradicting

Discussion: Contradictions and accusations put the speaker on the spot, and make it necessary for her or him to take a defensive position. They also say to the speaker, "You are wrong." or "You are bad."

Criticizing/Name-calling/Putting-down

Discussion: Criticism diminishes the speaker. Few of us want to continue a conversation in which we are being diminished. Name-calling and put-downs are frequently veiled in humor, but may nonetheless be hurtful and damaging to a relationship.

Use these discussion questions after each communication stopper to expand the understanding of each one.

Discussion Questions:

1. What effect does this type of response have on the speaker? ...on the conversation? ...on the relationship?
2. Has this ever happened to you? What did you say and/or do?
3. Under what circumstances would it be okay to respond like this?
4. How could this communication stopper contribute to conflict?

Extension:

Have the students form teams of two. Assign one, or more, of the communication stoppers to each team. Have the teams create a role-play demonstrating their stopper(s). Ask each team to role-play for the entire group.

The Communication Stoppers
Experience Sheet

Have you ever tried to have a conversation with someone who wouldn't let you finish a sentence? Have you ever attempted to discuss a problem with someone who had an answer for everything? Bad communication habits can stop a conversation short. Here are a few to avoid:

Interrupting

Interruptions are the most common cause of stalled communication. It's frustrating to be interrupted in the middle of a sentence, and when interruptions happen over and over again, talking begins to feel like a waste of time.

Advising

Few people enjoy getting unasked-for advice. Statements that begin with, "Well, if I were

you...," or "If you ask me...," are like red flags. Advice-giving says, "I'm superior. I know better than you do." Advice can also cause a person to feel powerless—as though she can't make a good decision on her own.

Judging

When you tell people that their ideas or feelings are wrong, you are saying in effect that you know more than they do. If your ideas are drastically different from theirs, they'll either defend themselves (argue) or give up on the conversation. Even positive judgments like, "You're the smartest student in class," don't work if the person you're talking to doesn't *feel* very smart.

Interpreting

Some people develop a habit of analyzing everything (including statements) to reveal "deeper meanings." When you interpret or analyze, you imply an unwillingness to accept the speaker or the speaker's statements just as they are.

Dominating

We all know how frustrating and annoying it is to be in a conversation with someone who always has something better and more interesting to say than we do. In addition, when you dominate a conversation, others are forced to use another communication stopper, *interrupting*, just to get a word in.

Probing

Asking a lot of questions ("Why did you go there?" "Who did you see?" "What did he do?") tends to put the speaker on the defensive by requiring her to explain every statement. More importantly, your questions may lead the speaker *away from* what she originally wanted to say. If you ask too many questions, you are controlling, not sharing, the conversation.

Challenging/Accusing/Contradicting

There's nothing more frustrating than trying to talk with someone who challenges everything you say, insists that your ideas are wrong, or states that what happened was your fault. Contradictions and accusations put the speaker on the spot, and make the speaker defensive.

Criticizing/Name-calling/Put-downs

Don't make sarcastic or negative remarks in response to the things someone says. Criticism whittles away at self-esteem. Hardly anyone wants to continue a conversation that's making him feel bad or small. Even name-calling and put-downs that sound funny can still be hurtful. In the long run, they damage friendships.

The Active Listener
Communication Skill Practice

Objectives:
The students will:
— define the role of the listener in communication.
— identify and demonstrate "active listening" behaviors.

Materials:
a list of topics written on the whiteboard (see next page); one copy of the experience sheet, "How to Be An Active Listener," for each student

---

Directions:

Begin the session by asking the students what it feels like to be interrupted or to realize that someone they are talking to didn't hear a word they said. Then, ask how they feel when someone really listens to them.

Ask the students to describe what a good listener says and does to show that he or she is interested in what the speaker is saying and is really listening. Write their ideas on the whiteboard. Be sure to include these behaviors:

1. Face the speaker.
2. Look into the speaker's eyes without staring.
3. Be relaxed, but attentive.
4. Listen to the words and try to picture in your own mind what the speaker is telling you.
5. Don't interrupt or fidget. When it is your turn to respond, don't change the subject or start telling your own story.
6. If you don't understand something, wait for the speaker to pause and then ask, "What do you mean by..."

7. Try to feel what the speaker is feeling (show empathy).
8. Respond in ways that lets the speaker know that you are listening and understand what is being said. Ways of responding might include nodding, saying "uh huh," or giving feedback that proves you are listening, for example:

   • Briefly summarize: "You're saying that you might have to quit the team in order to have time for a job."
   • Restate feelings: "You must be feeling pretty bad." or "You sound really happy!"

Tell the students that this type of listening is called active listening. Ask them if they can explain why the word active is used to describe it.

Explain that today they will be practicing active listening, one of the most important communication skills they will ever learn.

Ask the students to form groups of three. Tell them to decide who is **A**, who is **B**, and who is **C**. Announce that you are going to give the students an opportunity to practice active listening. Explain the process: *In the first round, **A** will be the speaker and **B** will be the listener and will use active listening. **C** will be the observer. C's job is to notice how well B listens, and report his or her observations at the end of the round. I will be the timekeeper. We will have three rounds, so that you can each have a turn in all three roles. When you are the speaker, pick a topic from the list on the board, and remember to pause occasionally so that your partner can respond.*

Signal the start of the first round. Call time after 3 minutes. Have the observers give feedback for 1 minute. Tell the students to switch roles. Conduct two more rounds. Lead a follow-up discussion.

Distribute the experience sheets. Give the students time to complete them. Then lead a culminating discussion.

Discussion Questions:

1. How did it feel to "active listen?"
2. What was it like to be the observer?
3. When you were the speaker, how did you feel having someone really listen to you?
4. What was easiest about active listening? What was hardest?
5. What did you learn from your observer?
6. Why is it important to learn to be a good listener?
7. What role does good listening play in resolving disagreements or conflicts?
8. What do you need to do to become a better listener?

List of topics:

"A Time I Needed Some Help"

"Something I'd Like to Do Better"

"A Problem I Need to Solve"

"A Time I Got Into an Argument"

"A Time I Made a Tough Decision"

"Something I'd Like to Be or Do When I'm an Adult"

"My Favorite Thing to Do on a Saturday"

"My Favorite Movie"

"If I Could Have One Wish, It Would Be..."

"The Most Fun I've Ever Had"

How to Be An Active Listener
Experience Sheet

Listening is a very important part of good communication. Listed below are characteristics of a good listener. Check ones that describe you most of the time.

A good listener:

___ Faces the speaker.

___ Looks into the speaker's eyes, but doesn't stare.

___ Is relaxed, but attentive.

___ Keeps an open mind.

___ Listens to the words and tries to picture what the speaker is saying.

___ Doesn't interrupt or fidget.

___ Waits for the speaker to pause to ask clarifying questions.

___ Tries to feel what the speaker is feeling (shows empathy).

___ Nods and says "uh huh," or summarizes to let the speaker know he or she is listening.

What is your strongest quality as a listener?

_____

_____

_____

_____

What is your weakest quality as a listener?

_____

_____

_____

_____

How can you become a better listener?

_____

_____

_____

_____

Leading and Following
A Communications Experiment

Objectives:

The students will:
— practice communicating clearly and accurately.
— describe problems caused by imprecise communication and differing interpretations.

Materials:

one copy of the experience sheet, "A Day at the Zoo" for each student

---

Directions:

Distribute the experience sheets. Explain to the students that they are going to use the zoo map while participating in an activity that focuses on the importance of communicating clearly and accurately and listening carefully. Give the students a few minutes to become familiar with the map. Allow interaction during this process.

Next, ask a volunteer to bring his or her map and join you in front of the group. Have the volunteer choose a location on the map and tell everyone what it is. Make sure that all of the students find the correct location (starting point). Tell them to place the tip of their index finger or pencil on the location and listen for directions.

Instruct the volunteer to *silently choose* a destination on the map and, *without telling what the destination is*, give a series of directions for getting there. Tell the students to listen to the directions and use their finger or pencil to trace the route on their map.

After the last direction, ask the students: *Where are you?*

Allow the students to react. Use their comments and frustrations to generate a

brief discussion about the skills of speaking and listening accurately, and of giving and following clear directions. Then repeat the exercise several more times, with the help of additional volunteers. Lead a culminating discussion.

Discussion Questions:

1. How did you feel when you were giving directions?
2. How did you feel when you were following directions?
3. What specifically did you do to help your classmates understand your directions?
4. How can we communicate clear and exact messages?
5. Has anything like this ever happened to you? Tell us about a time when you had trouble getting a precise message across or correctly understanding someone else's message.
6. What have you learned about language and communication from this experiment?
7. When you are trying to resolve a conflict, why is it important to be very clear in your communication?

A Day At The Zoo

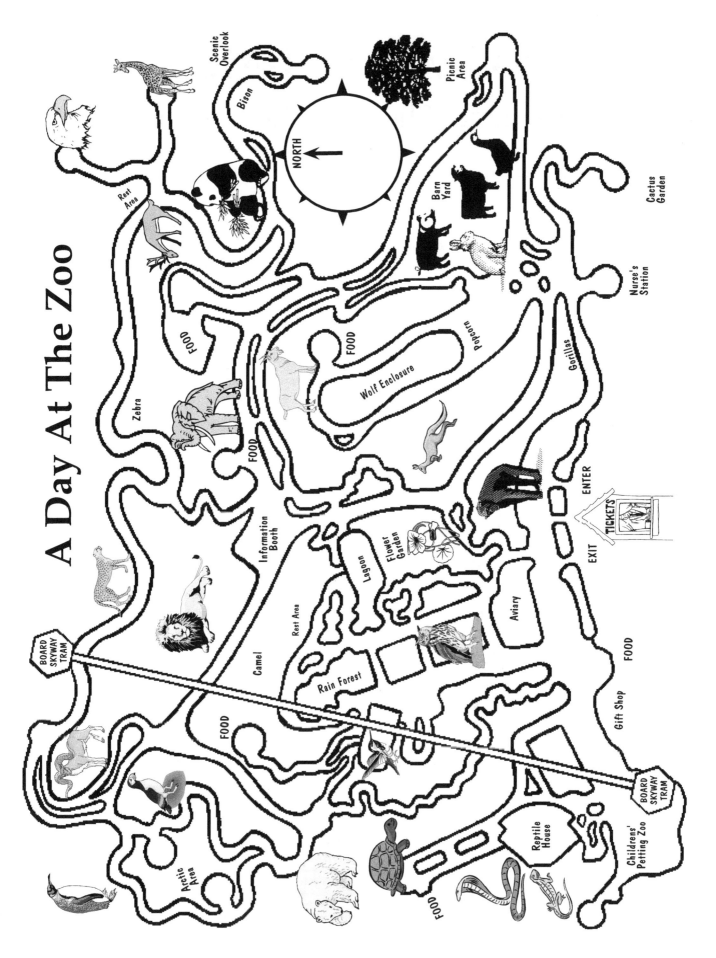

How to Give An "I-Message"
Experience Sheet and Discussion

Objectives:

The students will:
— compare "I" messages and "you" messages and describe their differences.
— identify the three parts of an "I" message.
— practice formulating "I" messages.

Materials:

one copy of the experience sheet, "Giving An 'I-Message'" for each student; whiteboard, or chart paper and magic marker

Procedure:

Tell the students that you want to talk with them about an effective, assertive strategy for responding to someone who has done something you don't like. In your own words, explain to the students: *When you are having a problem or conflict with someone, one of the most powerful messages you can send is an "I-message." An I-message tells the listener what the problem is, how you feel about it, and what you want (or don't want) the listener to do. Many times, we send You-messages when we would be much better off sending I-messages. You-messages are often blaming and threatening, frequently make the listener feel mad or hurt, usually make the problem worse, and many times don't even describe the problem. You-messages can even start a conflict where none existed before.*

I-messages get their name from the fact that they begin with the word, "I." When you use an I-message, you are talking about yourself. — your perceptions, your beliefs, your feelings, and your wishes.

I-messages are an effective way to talk to people when you are mad at them or frustrated by them. With an I-message, *you express your own concerns. In order to express them, you have to get in touch with them.*

When the listener hears an I-message, the listener knows that she or he has done something that you object to. The listener also knows that you feel badly about the behavior.

By using an I-message, you can convey a strong message without making the listener feel terrible or incapable. I-messages are a clear and non-threatening way to tell people what you want and how you feel.

On the board, write the following I-message formula:

1. **I feel _____**
2. **when you _____**
3. **and I want you to _____**

Provide several examples:

"I feel mad when you push in front of me in line, because I am very hungry and don't want to wait any longer to get my lunch. I need for you to get in line and wait your turn."

"I feel worried when you copy my paper, because I'm afraid we'll both get into trouble. I need you to complete your own work and not copy mine."

"I feel sad when you say things about me behind my back, because it makes me not trust you anymore. I hope you won't talk behind my back again."

Distribute the experience sheets. Go over the directions with the students. Provide time for the students to complete the experience sheet. Allow the students to work in pairs or small groups to do so.

Take one cartoon at a time, and ask two volunteers to demonstrate it by first role-playing the "you" message, and then their own "I" messages. Invite other members of the class to come forward, step into the role play, and substitute their own "I" message. Contrast the various efforts and discuss their effectiveness.

Discussion Questions:

1. What is the hardest part of composing an I-message?
2. How do you feel when someone gives you a You-message? ...an I-message?
3. How does an I-message communicate your angry feelings without making the problem worse?
4. Would you be more likely to change your behavior in response to a You-message or an I-message? ...Why?
5. How can using I-messages help us settle arguments and resolve conflicts?

Giving An "I-Message"
Experience Sheet

Good Communication is the Key!

When another person does something we don't like, we may be tempted to send the person a You-message. You-messages get their name from the fact that they often start with the word "you." They are blaming messages. They can make the other person feel mad or hurt—and they can make the situation worse.

Try using an I-message instead. I-messages talk about your feelings and needs. They can help the other person understand you. Here's how to make an I-message:

1. Say how you feel. *(I feel sad.)*

2. Describe the situation. *(I feel sad when you bully Sandra.)*

3. Describe what you want the person to do. *(I feel sad when you bully Sandra and I want you to stop being mean to her.)*

Now, you try it! Read the You-message in the first cartoon bubble. Then write a better message—an I-message—in the second bubble.

You're late again! You're so inconsiderate. I'm never going to plan to do anything with you ever again!

I feel _____ ,

when you _____

_____ , and I want you to _____

_____

_____

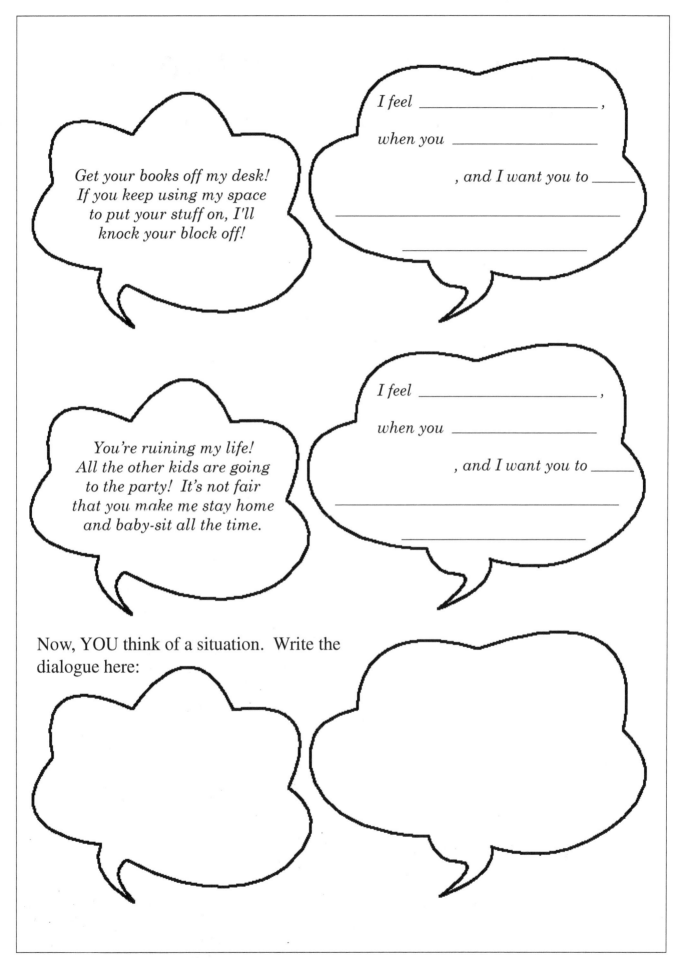

Get your books off my desk! If you keep using my space to put your stuff on, I'll knock your block off!

I feel _____,

when you _____

_____, and I want you to _____

_____

_____

You're ruining my life! All the other kids are going to the party! It's not fair that you make me stay home and baby-sit all the time.

I feel _____,

when you _____

_____, and I want you to _____

_____

_____

Now, YOU think of a situation. Write the dialogue here:

Understanding Body Language
Dramatizations and Discussion

Objectives:

The students will
— demonstrate that communication involves much more than the simple transmission of words and ideas.
— discuss how feelings are conveyed in communication.

Materials:

one copy of the experience sheet, "Your Body Talks, Too!," for each student

Directions:

Prior to class, write the following words on the board:

delight	confusion
surprise	worry
hate	sadness
love	irritation
anger	fear

Begin the activity by briefly reviewing the list of words with the students. Explain that these are just some of the many emotions people feel. Point out that communication involves much more than the simple use of words. Emotions get into the act in a number of ways.

Illustrate the point by silently selecting one of the emotions listed on the board and asking the class to guess which one it is while you repeat one of the tongue twisters listed. Say the tongue twister and, with your tone, inflection, facial expression, posture, and movements, simultaneously convey the emotion you selected. After the laughter subsides, allow the students to guess which emotion you were trying to convey. Then ask them how they knew. List the clues they mention on the board.

Repeat the tongue twister once or twice, conveying other emotions from the list. Discuss with the class the specific tones, inflection, facial expressions, body postures, and movements you used to express each feeling.

Invite the students to demonstrate other emotions. Have volunteers come to the front of the class and repeat the process. Introduce a new tongue twister from time to time. After each demonstration, ask the class to examine the manner in which the emotion was communicated. Ask questions such as:

1. Can you describe the tone and inflection?
2. What did his face do?
3. What was her posture like?
4 How did she move her body?

Tongue Twisters

- Rubber baby-buggy bumpers
- She sells sea shells by the sea shore.
- Peter Piper picked a peck of pickled peppers.
- How much wood would a woodchuck chuck if a woodchuck could chuck wood?
- Big black bugs bleed blood.

After some or all of the emotions listed have been demonstrated, vary the activity. Restrict what the performers can do. First, ask them not to move their bodies in any way, using words, tone, and inflection only. Second, ask them to convey the emotion completely nonverbally, depending only on facial expressions, posture, and body language.

Distribute the "Your Body Talks, Too!" experience sheet. Give the students a few minutes to fill it out. Lead a follow-up discussion.

Discussion Questions:

1. How do people communicate without words?
2. Why do you think tongue twisters were used in our dramatizations, instead of important ideas?
3. How can you hide your feelings when you are communicating with someone? What effect does that have on communication?
4. Why is it important to understand body language when you are trying to communicate important things to someone when you are in a conflict?
5. What did you learn from this activity? ...from the experience sheet?

Your Body Talks, Too!
Experience Sheet

You communicate with your body all the time. As you react emotionally to events in your life, your body takes on different postures and positions.

Think of a time recently when you experienced the following emotions. What did you do with your body? How do you think your body looked to others? Describe your body language below:

Embarrassment: _____
_____
_____

Nervousness: _____
_____
_____

Excitement: _____
_____
_____

Boredom: _____
_____
_____

Sadness: _____
_____
_____

Surprise _____
_____
_____

Fright: _____
_____
_____

How We Interact
A Social Skills Activity

Objectives:

The students will:
— describe the process by which social skills are learned.
— develop awareness concerning how to improve their own social skills.
— explain how good social skills facilitate effective conflict management.

Materials:

one copy of the "Social Skills Checklist" for each student

Directions:

Begin this activity by asking the students if they have ever felt awkward in a social situation. Share an experience of your own and invite the students to share their experiences. Using these illustrations as a lead-in, present the following facts about social skills—what they are and how we acquire them. Write key points on the board as you discuss them with the students. Encourage student comments and observations.

1. Social skills are abilities that help you take appropriate action in situations involving other people. Social skills also help you understand and appropriately respond to the actions of others.

2. Social skills include all of the different behaviors we use in social interactions—patterns of eye contact, facial expressions, gestures and voice characteristics, saying the right thing at the right time, using humor appropriately and so on.

3. A social skill, like any skill, can be learned and improved with practice.

4. Once learned, social skills become automatic.

5. All of us experience times when we are not sure how to behave. Managing these situations requires learning from observation.

Draw this diagram on the board

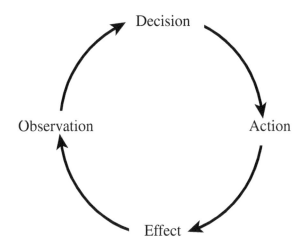

Explain that this is a diagram of how we learn appropriate behavior. This repeating cycle of *observation, decision, action,* and *effect* is fundamental to building social skills and no interaction takes place without it. In your own words, explain how it works:

You notice a person at a party you would like to talk to and you **observe** *that her behavior seems to indicate she is alone and would also like to have someone to talk with. You* **decide** *to break the ice by taking the* **action** *of making an introductory comment. This action has an* **effect** *on her which you* **observe** *and interpret before* **deciding** *what your next* **action** *will be. In the meantime, she has* **observed** *you making your introductory comment,* **decided** *how to respond,* **acted** *on that decision, and* **observed** *her* **effect** *on you. As the ice breaks, these interdependent cycles (yours and hers) become faster moving and more automatic.*

Point out that by observing the reactions of others to our behaviors and comments, we learn whether or not we are having the desired effect. This information allows us to adapt future behavior. Positive reactions reinforce our belief that we are acting appropriately. Unfavorable reactions alert us to the fact that we may have said or done something inappropriate.

At the conclusion of this presentation/ discussion, pass out copies of the "Social Skills Checklist" and review it with the students. Suggest that the students take some time to think through the different items and (as recommended) solicit feedback from others. Tell them that they can use this checklist as a reminder of which social skills they would like to enhance.

Next, ask the students to pair up. Explain that each person is to take 3 minutes to talk about a time he or she learned something important related to a social skill. Ask the students to describe the situation, what they were doing and/ or saying and what observation they made that led them to their learning. Keep time and have the partners switch roles at the end of 3 minutes.

After all students have had a chance to share, lead a culminating class discussion.

Discussion Questions:

1. How aware are you of consciously making decisions about what is appropriate behavior?
2. How do you explain the fact that some people seem to be more skilled in social situations than others?
3. Would you expect people with good social skills to be better at handling conflict situations? Explain.
4. What can you do to help yourself develop good social skills?

Social Skills Checklist
Experience Sheet

Improving your social skills is easier if you understand what effective interactions are all about. Below is a list of behaviors that people with good social skills use when they interact with others. Use this checklist to focus on specific social skills you possess and to consider which skills it would be a good idea to practice and improve Put a check (✔) next to the behaviors you usually use. Put an (X) next to those that could be improved. You may find some items more difficult than others to assess. Here are some helpful hints:

1. Pay attention to how you think you are doing.
2. Consciously observe how others react to your social behaviors.
3. Ask close friends or family members to give you their opinions.
4. Pinpoint one or two areas at a time to work on.

Nonverbal Behavior

Do you...

___ look at the person who is speaking?

___ smile or nod when you agree with what the speaker is saying?

___ stay focused on the speaker by facing him/her—not turning or looking away?

___ keep a comfortable distance between you and those with whom you are talking?

___ look into the other person's eyes a comfortable amount of time—not to much or too intently, and not to little?

___ use body language that matches what you are saying?

Voice Quality

Do you...

___ speak at the right volume—not too loudly or too softly for the circumstances?

___ use a variety of tones so that your voice is not dull or expressionless?

___ speak clearly?

___ speak at an appropriate rate—not too fast or too slow?

___ speak in a pleasant, even flow without repetition, stammering, omissions or long pauses?

Verbal Behavior

Do you...

___ say things that build on what others have said?

___ say things that encourage others to participate?

___ allow others to speak without interruption?

___ make statements that are not too long or too short?

___ express appropriate humor—not too much or at the wrong times?

___ take your turn to speak at appropriate times—neither staying quiet for long periods nor dominating the conversation?

___ ask questions that are appropriate (not off the subject, not too probing or personal)?

A Time I Remember Feeling...
Dyad Sequence and Discussion

Objectives:
The students will:
— discuss their feelings as they relate to specific topics.
— begin to understand that all people experience the same feelings, but in different ways.

Materials:
one copy of the experience sheet, "Feel Your Feelings," for each student; whiteboard, or chart paper and markers

Directions:
Select 10 to 12 feeling words from the following list and write them along with the heading on the board or chart paper. Choose words that are appropriate for the age and maturity of your students.

"A Time I Remember Feeling...
...Angry"
...Free"
...Suspicious"
...Curious"
...Amused"
...Jealous"
...Shocked"
...Appreciated"
...Uneasy"
...Scared"
...Left Out"
...Self-conscious"
...Confident"
...Overwhelmed"
...Guilty"
...Surprised"
...Worthless"
...Optimistic"
...Confused"
...Unfairly Treated"
...Lonely"
...Annoyed"
...Relieved"

...Homesick"
...Loved"
...Disgusted"
...Shy"
...Embarrassed"
...Bored"
...Helpless"
...Delighted"
...Depressed"
...Powerful"
...Peaceful"
...Inspired"
...Pessimistic"
...Happy"
...Cynical"

Introduce the activity by telling the students that they are going to have an opportunity to discuss a number of feelings that they experience. Have the students form groups of four and spread out to various areas of the room. If necessary, join a group yourself or have one group of six; however, make sure all groups contain an even number of students.

Explain to the students that they will be involved in a dyad sequence in which they will talk one-to-one with each member of their group for about 3 minutes concerning a feeling.

Ask the students to pair up with one member of their group. When the dyads are formed, ask the students to decide who will speak first and who will speak second, and to choose a feeling topic from the list on the board. Tell the students that they will each have 1 1/2 minutes to speak to that topic. Ask the first speakers to begin. At the end of 1 1/2 minutes, signal the students to switch roles so that the second speaker can address the same topic for another 1 1/2 minutes.

At the end of the first round, have the students change partners. This is easily accomplished by asking the students who spoke first to remain seated while the students who listened first move to a new partner within their group.

Repeat the process for each subsequent round, continuing until every student has had a dyad discussion with every other person in his or her group. Ask the students to return to their regular seating.

Distribute the experience sheets and give the students time to complete them. (As an alternative, request that the students complete their sheets as homework.)

Encourage everyone to participate in a culminating discussion.

Discussion Questions:

1. What did you notice or learn as you talked about these feelings with your partners?
2. When it comes to feelings, in what ways are you like one or more of your partners? In what ways are your feelings different?
3. What questions or ideas did you have while completing the experience sheet?
4. Why do people have different feelings in response to the same event?
5. What did you learn about yourself during this activity that you would feel okay sharing with us?

Feel Your Feelings
Experience Sheet

Your feelings are similar to the feelings of other people. Yet you are a one-of-a-kind person. Things that cause you to feel a certain way may cause an entirely different reaction in others. You are not exactly like everyone else.

The following exercise will help you get in touch with some of your feelings. As you write, keep in mind that *everyone* has these feelings. Feelings can be pleasant and unpleasant. But they are not good or bad. They are not right or wrong. Feelings just are!

I am happy when... _____

_____

I become angry when... _____

_____

I am sad when... _____

_____

I get scared when... _____

_____

I feel lonely when... _____

_____

I feel peaceful when... _____

_____

I become frustrated when... _____

_____

I hate it when... _____

_____

I love it when... _____

_____

What Goes Into a Decision?
Experience Sheet and Discussion

Objectives:

The students will:
— describe and analyze a recent decision.
— discuss factors that affect decision making.
— explain how to increase alternatives during decision making.

Materials:

one copy of the experience sheet, "Thinking of Alternatives," for each student; whiteboard or chart paper

Directions:

Begin the activity by presenting concepts related to decision making. Elicit contributions from the students and write notes on the board, as you make the following points:

1. A decision is not necessary unless there is more than one course of action to choose from.
2. Not deciding is making a decision.
3. Learning decision-making skills increases the possibility that you can have what you want.
4. Each decision is limited by what you are *able* to do. For example, if you cannot drive a car, you cannot choose between walking and driving.
5. The more alternatives you know about, the more you are *able* to do. For example, if you are unaware of a particular college, you cannot include it among your alternatives when deciding where to go to school.
6. Each decision is also limited by what you are *willing* to do.
7. What you are *willing* to do is usually determined by your values, beliefs, preferences, and past experiences.

Distribute the experience sheet, "Thinking of Alternatives." Go over the items on the sheet and answer any questions. Then give the students time to complete the sheet. Circulate and offer ideas and suggestions on how they can increase their alternatives.

Have the students form small groups and share their responses. When they have finished, lead a culminating class discussion.

Discussion Questions:

1. What did you learn about decision making from this activity?
2. What can you do to increase your alternatives in a decision-making situation?
3. What kinds of things determine your willingness to try a particular alternative?
4. When your willingness is more a product of low self-confidence than of values, how can you overcome that roadblock?
5. How do your beliefs affect decision making? Your attitudes? Your previous experiences?
6. Does resolving a conflict involve making decisions? What kinds of decisions?

31

Thinking of Alternatives
Experience Sheet

Think of a decision you need to make. Describe it here: _____

_____

_____

What are you able to do in this situation? Write down as many realistic alternatives as you can think of. The more alternatives you know about, the more you are able to do.

_____   _____

_____   _____

_____   _____

Go back and circle all of the alternatives you are willing to try.

One of the best ways to increase your chances of making a good decision is to increase your alternatives. Write down as many ideas as you can think of for increasing your alternatives. Where can you go for more information regarding the decision you need to make, and who can you ask for help?

1._____

2._____

3._____

4._____

5._____

6._____

7._____

8._____

9._____

10._____

Remember: In decision making, information is your biggest ally.

How to Make A Decision
Experience Sheet and Discussion

Objectives:

The students will:
— understand and describe how decisions are influenced.
— develop and practice a process for effective decision making.

Materials:

one copy of the experience sheet, "The Decision-Making Process," for each student; whiteboard or chart paper

Directions:

Distribute the experience sheets. Read through the decision-making steps with the students, examining each one. Here are some suggestions to discuss and questions to ask:

• (Step 2) Knowing what is important to you and what you want to accomplish involves such things as likes/dislikes, values, and interests. Most important, it involves having goals.

• (Step 3) You can get information by using the internet, talking to people, visiting places, watching TV, and reading. Once you have the information, you must be able to evaluate it. If two people tell you to do opposite things, how are you going to know which is right? What if neither is right? What if both are right? How do you know that what you find on the internet is true?

• (Step 5) Look into the future. Ask yourself what would be the probable outcome for each of the alternatives available.

Practice looking into the future with the students by asking them to predict their future based on these questions:

What would happen if:
— you did not go to college?
— you never got married?
— you dropped out of school?
— you became temporarily disabled?
— you became a professional rock singer?
— you decided never to drink alcohol?
— you decided not to have children?
— you became permanently disabled?

How did you make your predictions? What information did you use?

• (Step 6) When you reach the decision point, don't procrastinate. If you've done a good job on the other steps, you can choose the best alternative with confidence. Remember, if you don't choose, someone else may choose for you.

• (Step 7) Not every decision requires an action plan, but the big ones usually do. The decision to attend a 4-year college in another state won't come true unless you make it. And that means developing an action plan.

Give the students time to complete the experience sheet. (If you run out of time, let them complete it as homework.)

Have the students choose partners
and take turns sharing their decisions
and decision-making process. Facilitate a
culminating discussion.

Discussion Questions:

1. What did you learn about decision-
   making from this activity?
2. What can happen if you put off
   making a decision?
3. Why is it important to know your
   interests and values when making
   decisions?
4. How can having goals help you make
   decisions?

The Decision-Making Process
Experience Sheet

*The decision-making process involves using what you know (or can learn)
to get what you want.*

Here are some steps to follow when you have a decision to make:
1. Recognize and define the decision to be made.
2. Know what is important to you—your values—and what you want to accomplish—your goal.
3. Study the information you have already; obtain and study new information, too.
4. List all of your alternatives.
5. List the advantages and disadvantages of each alternative.
6. Make a decision.
7. Develop a plan for carrying out your decision.

Now let's see how the process really works.

1. **Think of a decision that you need to make. Define it here:**

   _____

   _____

2. **What is your goal relative to this decision?**

   _____

   What kinds of things that are important in your life
   (your values) might affect, or be affected by,
   this decision?

   _____

   _____

   _____

35

3. What kinds of information do you have or need?

Things to think about: _____ **Things to read:** _____

_____ _____

_____ _____

People to talk to: _____ **Things to do:** _____

_____ _____

_____ _____

4. & 5. What are your alternatives and what are the advantages and disadvantages of each?

Alternative #1	
Advantages	Disadvantages
Alternative #2	
Advantages	Disadvantages
Alternative #3	
Advantages	Disadvantages

Decision Point!
6. Which alternative has the best chance of producing the outcome you want?

_____

7. Now that you've made a decision, you need to develop a plan for putting that decision into action. Use the space below to describe each step you need to take and when you plan to achieve it.

This Is the Plan

Steps:	When?
1.	
2.	
3.	
4.	
5.	
6.	

Responsible Decision Making
Experience Sheet and Discussion

Objectives:

The students will:
— examine the elements of choice and responsibility in decision making.
— describe decisions involving frustration, procrastination, and risk.

Materials:

one copy of the experience sheet, "Making Wise Decisions," for each student; whiteboard or chart paper

Directions:

Distribute the experience sheets. Explain to the students that you want them to read the different situations and answer the questions. Give the students about 15 minutes to complete the sheet. Than have them form groups of three to five, and share their responses to the questions.

After the groups have finished sharing, facilitate a class discussion. Focus on the elements of responsibility and choice in decision making.

Discussion Questions:

1. Why is it sometimes difficult to take the initiative concerning decisions that affect us?
2. When you were a child, your parents or guardians made many decisions for you. What effect might that have on your ability to assume responsibility for decision making now?
3. What kind of decision is "putting off" or not making a decision?
4. When you have to choose between two equally attractive alternatives, how can you weigh them more carefully?
5. Some people love to make decisions that involve big risks. Others like to play it safe. How can you determine how much risk is right for you, so that you won't get in over your head?
6. When making decisions, how important is it to be responsible to your own needs and values?... to the needs and values of other people?
7. What is the most difficult part of decision making?... the easiest?
8. What have you learned about decision making that will help you in future decisions that you will have to make?

Making Wise Decisions
Experience Sheet

Dan starts a class he doesn't enjoy much, and after a couple of days he says to himself, "I'm not interested in anything being covered in this class. I don't have to take it to graduate, so I'm going to transfer to a class that I'll be able to use, one that I'll enjoy." And he does.

Maria has similar feelings about a class. But after thinking it over, she decides that since the class is in her major field of interest, she'll stick with it. As the semester continues, Maria finds that the class gets more interesting.

Suzanne feels the same way about a class she signed up for, but doesn't transfer to another one. She doesn't want to disappoint her parents or cause anyone to think she isn't capable of handling the class.

Dan, Suzanne, and Maria all face a similar situation, but each reacts differently. Suzanne's decision is based on what she imagines other people will think, rather than her own needs. Dan and Maria decide to do different things, but both of them make thoughtful decisions based on their own needs and values.

Think of a decision you made recently that worked out well.

What was it? _____

_____

Who and/or what influenced your decision?

___ Your needs (things you can't get along without)

___ Your values (what you like)

___ Your goals (what you want to accomplish)

___ Advertising

Other people... *Who?* _____

_____

___ Other... What? _____

_____

_____

Sometimes making decisions can be frustrating.

For weeks, Ryan has been working on his car. He has spent all his money and every available hour getting it fixed up for a custom car show. Now, the day before the show, some of his friends invite him to go with them to the river tomorrow. Ryan really enjoys going to the river, but he wants to enter his car in the show, too. Both things are happening on the same day. It makes him mad that he has to choose between two things he wants.

Has anything like this ever happened to you? How did you feel at the time?

_____

_____

What did you do?

_____

_____

_____

_____

Sometimes we decide not to decide.

The coach asks Tom if he wants to be on the track team, which makes Tom feel great, except that he is nervous about being the newest and least experienced person on the team. So Tom puts off making a decision. Accidentally (on purpose) he forgets to let the coach know by the deadline. A day or two later Tom says to himself, "Too bad I forgot about notifying Coach that I wanted to be on the track team. Oh, well."

Have you ever put off making a decision? If you could get that day back, what would you do this time?

_____

_____

_____

_____

_____

_____

Sometimes decisions are risky.

Sheila thinks she wants to go to college, but she isn't sure what it will be like. She's been planning to go to a nearby community college for two years while continuing to live at home. Then she finds out that she could live with her aunt in the city and go to a well-known four-year college. Sheila doesn't know if she really wants to leave home yet, if she wants to live with her aunt, or which college will be the better choice.

What do you think Sheila should do?

___ Live at home and go to the community college.

___ Live with her aunt and go to the four-year college.

___ Get a lot more information before making a decision.

What types of information does Sheila need?

List **at least** four categories of information that will be of value to her.

Sheila needs know about...

1. _____

2. _____

3. _____

4. _____

Others: _____

_____

_____

Try this:

Next time you watch a movie or TV show, notice the decisions the characters in the story make. You will probably think some of the decisions are reasonable and others will seem wrong or foolish. See if you can analyze how each decision was made.

Problem-Solving Steps
Experience Sheet and Discussion

Objectives:

The students will:
— understand and describe how decisions are influenced.
— develop and practice a process for effective problem solving.

Materials:

one copy of the experience sheet, "Steps for Solving a Problem Responsibly," for each student; whiteboard or chart paper

---

Directions:

Distribute the experience sheet, "Steps for Solving a Problem Responsibly." Have the students read each step in the problem-solving process with you while writing notes on their sheet. Generate discussion after each step by asking the questions below and other open-ended questions. As an elaboration of the process, introduce a personal example (a problem that you need to solve) and take it through the process as part of the discussion. If time permits, go back through the process a second time, using as an example a problem described by one of the students.

Discussion Questions:

1. Stop all blaming

1. What happens when you get bogged down in the blaming game?
2. What are people who constantly blame others for their problems trying to avoid?
3. How is blaming others the same as giving away your power?

2. Define the problem

1. Why is it so important to know exactly what the problem is?
2. Why does it matter whether it's your problem or someone else's?
3. When should people not be left to solve their own problems?
4. What can happen when a person gets all worked up about a problem that isn't even his or hers?

3. Consider asking for help

1. When is it wise to ask for help?
2. Who gets to decide what kind of help you need?
3. If what you want is information or advice, and instead the person tries to solve the problem for you, what can you do?

4. Think of alternative solutions.

1. What is the advantage of thinking of alternatives?
2. If you can't think of more than one or two alternatives, what should you definitely do before making a decision?
3. How does collecting information expand your alternatives?

5. *Evaluate the alternatives.*

1. What are some ways of collecting information?
2. Why not just do the first thing that comes to mind?
3. Why is it important to imagine what will happen as a result of trying each alternative?

6. *Make a decision.*

If you still can't make a decision, which steps in the process could you return to? (2., 4., 5., and 3., in that order. The problem may be incorrectly defined; you may need to gather additional information; the consequences may need further consideration; or help may be called for.)

7. *Follow through*

1. Why stick to a decision?
2. What can you do if the solution doesn't work or more problems come up?
3. How can you evaluate your decision?
4. What's an example of a big problem in our society that used to be a much smaller problem with a relatively easy solution?

Steps for Solving a Problem Responsibly
Experience Sheet

What is a problem?

A problem can be a complicated issue or question that you have to answer.   Or it can be something in your life that is causing you frustration, worry, anger, or some other kind of distress. In order to answer the question or get rid of the distress, you must "solve" the problem.   Problems often have several parts. Solving the whole problem involves making a series of decisions — at least one decision for each part of the problem.

Next time you are faced with a problem, follow these steps to a solution:

---

1. Stop all blaming.
   It will help me to understand that blaming someone (including myself) for the problem will not solve it. If I really want to solve the problem, I need to put my energy into working out a solution. Blaming myself and others is a waste of time.

---

2. Define the problem.
   Next, I need to ask myself two questions to help me get started. "What exactly is the problem?" and "Whose problem is it?" If I find that it's not my problem, the best thing I can do is let the people who "own" the problem solve it themselves. Or I can ask them, "How can I help you?"

3. Consider asking for help.

Once I'm sure I "own" the problem and know what it is, I may choose to ask someone for help. For example, I may decide to talk over the problem with someone.

4. Think of alternative solutions.

I need to ask myself, "What are some things I could do about this?" I need to think of as many reasonable ideas for solving the problem as I can. To do this, I will probably need to collect some information.

5. Evaluate the alternatives.

Next, for each idea I come up with, I need to ask myself, "What will happen to me and the other people involved if I try this one?" I need to be very honest with myself. If I don't know how someone else will be affected, I need to ask that person, "How will you feel about it if I..."

6. Make a decision.

I need to choose the alternative that appears to have the best chance of succeeding. If my solution is a responsible one, it will not hurt anyone unnecessarily— and it will probably work.

7. Follow through.

After I've made the decision, I'll stick to it for a reasonable length of time. If the decision doesn't work, I'll try another alternative. If the decision works, but causes more problems in the process, I'll start all over again to solve them. And I'll try not to blame myself or anybody else for those problems.

Have A Heart!
Decision-Making Exercise

Objectives:

The students will:
— make a shared decision concerning a difficult issue.
— describe their shared decision-making process.
— describe how values and attitudes affect decision making.

Materials:

one copy of the "Patient Waiting List" for each small group; writing materials

Directions:

Announce that the students are going to have an opportunity to make group decisions concerning a highly-charged, imaginary situation in which individual values and attitudes may play a significant role.

Ask the students to form groups of five to seven. Give each group a copy of the "Patient Waiting List," and suggest that every group choose a recorder.

Read the situation and the list of patients to the groups:

Situation:

You are surgeons at a large hospital. Your committee must make a very important decision. Seven patients need a heart transplant. There is only one heart donor at this time. All of the patients are eligible to receive the heart. All are physically able. And all have compatible blood and tissue typing. Which patient would you choose to receive the heart? Why? Your committee must agree on the choice.

(Be sure to acknowledge that recipients of organ transplants are now managed by a nationwide computer network, which removes such difficult decisions from the hands of the surgeons themselves. Ask the students to participate as if such a system had not yet been developed. Also, remind the students that patients who do not receive this heart will not automatically die. Some (not all) will survive until another donor is available.)

Refrain from giving any further instructions or suggestions. Allow at least 20 minutes for decision making. Then reconvene the class and question each group about its decision and its decision-making process. Facilitate discussion.

Discussion Questions:

1. What was your decision?
2. How did you arrive at your decision.
3. What decision-making method did you use (consensus, voting, etc.)?
4. How was your decision influenced by your values? ...your attitudes? ...your prejudices?
5. Who provided leadership in your group?
6. How were disagreements and conflicts handled?
7. How satisfied are you with your own level of participation in this exercise?

Patient Waiting List:

- 31-year-old male; Black; brain surgeon at the height of his career; no children

- 12-year-old female; Vietnamese; accomplished violinist

- 40-year-old male; Hispanic; teacher; two children

- 15 year female; White; unmarried; 6-months pregnant

- 35-year-old male; Hispanic; Roman Catholic priest

- 17-year-old female; White; waitress; high school dropout; supports/cares for a brother who is severely disabled

- 38-year-old female, White, AIDS researcher, no children

Understanding the Nature of Conflict

In order to develop healthy, confident attitudes toward conflict and conflict resolution, students need to examine its nature — what it is, how it is born, how it grows, and how it dies. They need to face their prejudices and fears about conflict and see conflict for what it is — a necessary and normal process that can have positive or negative results, depending on how it is handled.

The activities in this section help students define conflict, identify common sources of conflict, and become aware of vocabulary and body language that tend to escalate and de-escalate conflict. The students are helped to recognize that most people respond to most conflicts with the same learned patterns of behavior, and each student assesses and evaluates the effectiveness of his or her own conflict style. As an alternative to the use of *unconscious* conflict styles, the students consider the value of developing a repertoire of *conscious* conflict strategies. Finally, students learn to differentiate between assertive, aggressive, and passive behaviors and understand how these behaviors tend to affect the life cycle of a conflict.

I Think Conflict Is...
Word Association and Discussion

Objectives:

The students will:
— understand that conflict is a natural process of living.
— become aware that conflict is neither good nor bad, but that the result or consequence of conflict can be good or bad.
— develop a personal definition of conflict.

Materials —

dictionaries, paper, marking pens, and a copy of the "Conflict Consequences Chart" for each group

Information to share:

In addition to the negative outcomes we commonly associate with conflict, conflict produces some wonderful consequences if it is well managed. For instance, much creativity flows from conflict. Relationships are strengthened when conflict is handled effectively, and trust is either strengthened or diminished depending on the quality of conflict management. If possible, allow the students to discover and verbalize these concepts themselves in the course of the activity. Be sure that the positive aspects of conflict receive your focus. For other ideas, refer to the example on the "Conflict Consequences Chart" (next page).

Directions:

Ask the students to share as many synonyms for the word *conflict* as they can come up with. Write these on the board or on a chart pad.

Here is a partial list you can use as a reference:

Friction	Hassle	Problem
War	Belligerence	Confrontation
Clash	Battle	Fight

Violence	Disharmony	Row
Struggle	Collision	Strife

With the students, examine each word and determine if it is a positive word or a negative word. (Because conflict has a generally negative connotation, don't be surprised if all the words are negative.)

Explain to the students that conflict is something we all have to deal with. In your own words, say: *Conflict is a natural part of living. We all experience conflict from time to time simply because we are so different. Sometimes we have conflicts that don't involve other people. For example, when we have to make a tough decision, we may experience a personal or internal conflict as we try to decide between competing alternatives. Most people think of conflict as negative, but really it isn't negative or positive, it's just a process. Only the <u>outcomes</u> or <u>consequences</u> of conflict are good or bad. If we handle conflict skillfully, we can produce far more positive results than we can if we don't know what conflict is or how to handle it.*

Depending on the list, select one of the following approaches:

- If the list is more negative than positive, generate a discussion by asking the students why they think conflict is thought of as being bad.

- If the list is balanced or has more positive words, ask how it is that most other people view conflict as being negative.

If you are working with an entire class, ask the students to break into groups of five or six. Have each group select a recorder/reporter, and supply each group with a copy of the "Conflict Consequences Chart."

Next, have each group brainstorm and record in the left-hand column of its chart as many negative outcomes of conflict as can be thought of. (Suggest some examples on the model below to help them get started.)

Have the recorders/reporters read their group's list to the class.

After all of the groups have shared, have the groups return to their charts and fill in the right-hand column by instructing them to consider each negative outcome and record a corresponding positive outcome likely to result if a conflict is handled effectively.

Ask each group's recorder/reporter to share just a couple of examples by first giving the negative outcome and then the corresponding positive outcome.

After the sharing, ask the entire class what produces the difference between a negative and positive outcome to a conflict. Accept all responses. Make sure the students recognize that the difference between a negative and positive outcome is a function of the quality of conflict management.

Use this example to help your students.

Conflict Consequences Chart

Unmanaged Conflict = Negative Results	Well-Managed Conflict = Positive Results
Slows learning	Promotes learning and growth
Damages relationships	Strengthens relationships
Discourages cooperation	Stimulates and reinforces cooperation
Destroys trust	Builds trust and dialogue
Focuses on blaming and fault-finding	Produces sense of responsibility
Creates enemies and hard feelings	Strengthens relationships
Generates hostility and violence	Promotes peace and harmony

Discussion Questions:

1. Why is it important to have good conflict management skills?
2. In what ways do you see conflict differently than you did before?
3. How can conflict be a useful tool in building relationships and being more creative?

Extension:

Note: The following may also be used as a separate activity.

When your students have grasped the importance of having good conflict management skills and realize that conflict is just as likely to produce good results as bad, give them an opportunity to develop their own definition of conflict.

Using dictionaries as guides, ask the students in each group to develop a new definition for conflict incorporating their awareness of conflict as a process whose outcomes can range from negative to positive depending on the quality of its management.

Have each group's reporter share the new definition with everyone.

Discussion Questions:

1. Thinking of your new definitions of conflict, what needs to happen to ensure that conflicts have fewer negative and more positive outcomes?
2. What kinds of things cause conflicts?
3. What makes conflict worse? ...better?
4. How can understanding that conflict can have either good or bad outcomes help you handle your own conflicts better?

Conflict Consequences Chart
Experience Sheet

Unmanaged Conflict = Negative Results	Well-Managed Conflict = Positive Results

The Conflict Map
Idea Mapping and Discussion

Objectives:

The students will:
— create an idea map which demonstrates that conflict affects all aspects of living.
— see that all conflicts have certain things in common.
— learn that it is easier to manage conflict than it is to control all the people, places, and things that produce conflict.

Materials:

whiteboard

Information to Share:

An "idea map" is a way of recording and organizing information. Idea maps are less structured than outlines or lists, and allow us to see ideas in new contexts and relationships. Every idea is included because every idea has value.

Directions:

Announce that the students are going to have an opportunity to create a "map" showing what conflict means to them. Invite everyone to participate and to be as creative as possible.

Note: Since conflict is so intimately connected with every part of our lives, every idea that the students have is valuable and worth including. As the idea map develops, *every* idea that's offered, no matter how strange it may seem, should be included. For the student who offers it, it has meaning.

In the middle of the board, write the word "CONFLICT," and draw a circle around it.

Ask the students to think about their understanding of conflict and to take a moment to reflect on what the word means to them. Suggest they pay attention to anything that comes to mind when they think about conflict, including associations, feelings, and memories.

Ask for some examples, and record everything you hear. Each time an idea is offered, draw a solid line away from the circle in the center and write the word or phrase suggested at the end of the line.

As students offer ideas related to those already written on the map, begin to link these new ideas in appropriate ways to the thoughts previously suggested.

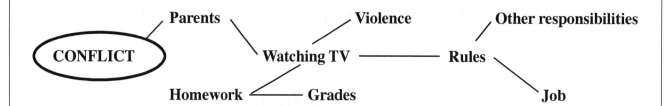

Encourage the students to make as many connections as they can to people, places, and things that they associate with conflict, and to the qualities in these items that tend to produce conflict.

Continue developing the map as long as time permits, or as long as interest remains high.

Discussion Questions:

1. In what ways does our idea map validate our definitions of conflict? In what ways does it suggest that we need to change our definitions?

2. What ingredients do all conflicts seem to have in common?

3. What things seem to determine the quality (good or bad) of a conflict's results?

4. As you look at our idea map of conflict, what does it tell you about the "relationships" of conflict? Do you think a conflict is an isolated event or is it the result of many related events?

5. How can understanding all the different things that affect a conflict help you to manage it better?

Discovering Sources of Conflict

Investigation, Sharing, and Discussion

Objectives:

The students will:
— discover that all conflicts, from personal to global, stem from a set of common sources.
— become aware of how differing perceptions and divergent points of view are a primary sources of conflict.
— develop a better understanding of the things that pull people into conflict.
— discuss how recognizing and appreciating different perceptions can be used to diffuse conflict.

Materials:

recent editions of local newspapers, and/or access to internet news sources, and/or copies of national news magazines; marking pens and one or two sheets of chart paper for each work group; masking tape

Note:

This is a two-part activity that can be done in one or two sessions, depending on available time.

Information to Share:

All conflicts, big and small, can be traced to a set of common sources (issues, concerns). These sources of conflict need to be understood so students recognize that to experience conflict is normal, but to manage it effectively takes skill and practice.

Directions (Part One):

On the board write the following list, leaving room on the right to place check marks:

Sources of Conflict (The Big 6)

Possessions
Environment
Opinions
Methods (Ways of doing things)
Beliefs
Control

Have the students form work groups of six to eight. Distribute the chart paper, marking pens, and a newspaper and/or magazine to each group, or if computers are available, you can have students use online news sources. Instruct the groups to identify five or six different conflicts that have been written about recently. **Important:** Remind the students that conflicts can range from simple disputes to wars, but that most conflicts don't involve violence.

Have the groups rank the conflicts they select from the most global to the most local (closest to home). Tell them to write brief one-line descriptions of the conflicts on a sheet of chart paper in the order in which they ranked them.

Ask each group to display its list and briefly describe the conflicts/articles chosen to the rest of the class. (Expect some duplication in the selections of the different groups.) Immediately after each group has shared, refer the group to the "Sources of

Conflict" list on the board. Ask the group to identify at least one source of conflict for each of its listed news articles, using the headings you have on the board. Each time a heading is chosen, put a check mark after that heading.

To assist the students you may want to briefly explain each heading as follows:

Possessions:
Things you own or think are yours. This includes your personal space.

Environment:
Places we are compelled to be. School is an example (if it is pleasant and fun there is no conflict; if we don't like it, there may be conflict).

Opinions:
Everyone has them and sometimes others don't agree.

Methods:
(Ways of doing things.) Very often someone thinks there is a better way. Sometimes you think there is a better way, but have to do it someone else's way.

Beliefs:
When you have a different belief than someone else, and you think you are right and the other person is wrong.

Control:
When individuals or groups struggle for control of an issue, situation, other people, territory, etc.

When the last group has contributed, point out the variety of conflict sources represented in the articles the class selected.

Next, ask the work groups to get back together, pulling their chairs or desks into a circular formation. Instruct the members to take turns briefly describing a recent (or current) *personal* conflict. Caution the students to keep their descriptions brief (1-minute), and to avoid using names or giving intimate details of the conflict. Ask them, as part of their sharing, to identify the root of their conflict from the "Sources

of Conflict" list on the board. Suggest that a recorder in each group make a list of the sources identified.

Allow 10-15 minutes for sharing. Then ask each group to report its breakdown of sources to the class. Using a different color marker, make additional check marks next to those already recorded on the board. Again, point out the variety of different sources.

Discussion Questions:

1. In what ways do global/national/local conflicts and our personal conflicts differ? In what ways are they the same?
2. Regardless of the sources, what are the primary reasons we have conflict? (different perceptions/points of view)
3. How does understanding that people share the same conflict sources, but have differing perceptions, help us deal with conflict more effectively?

Directions (Part Two) —

On a piece of chart paper, write the following statement in print large enough for the entire class to see:

FINISHED FILES ARE THE RESULT OF YEARS OF SCIENTIFIC EXPERIENCE COMBINED WITH THE EXPERIENCE OF MANY YEARS.

Tape another piece of chart paper over the statement to conceal it.

Explain to the students that they are going to experience how easily conflicts can arise. In your own words, explain that two or more people can be looking at exactly the same thing (e.g., a problem, a question, a statement, etc.) and see it differently. As we grow older, the way we see things in our world is determined more and more by our previous experiences and learnings. *Very often, conflict occurs when people start to argue about the different ways they perceive or see things.*

Generate a discussion by asking some of the following questions or others you think of:

— *What kinds of things do you see or perceive differently from someone else?*
— *What happens when people argue about their different perceptions?*
— *Have you ever thought you were right about something and then learned later that you were wrong? How did it happen? How did you feel about changing your mind?*
— *What do you think is the biggest reason people fight about things?*

Next, uncover the statement you previously wrote on chart paper, and ask the class to carefully read it and to count the number of "F"s in the statement. Give them about thirty seconds to do this and then recover the statement.

Ask the class to indicate by a show of hands how many counted just three (3) "F"s in the statement. Make a count and record the number on the board. Ask how many people saw just four (4) "F"s in the statement and record that number on the board. Repeat this process for five and six "F"s. Note that although everyone was looking at the same statement, people perceived it differently.

Again uncover the statement and ask the students to recount the number of "F"s. Allow about thirty seconds, recover the statement and then repeat the polling. Although the numbers will change, there will still be disparity. Point out that even after two chances everyone still doesn't perceive the statement the same way.

Uncover the statement once again and with the class count the number of "F"s in the statement. (There are six (6) "F"s in the statement)

Discussion Questions —

1. How do you explain the fact that we can look at the same thing and see it differently?
2. How does this exercise help you better understand the sources of conflict?
3. What have you learned about how conflicts get started?

The Language of Conflict
Media Investigation and Experience Sheet

Objectives:

Students will:
— apply knowledge of four types of conflict to real-life situations.
— begin building a conflict-related vocabulary.
— discuss how using peaceful words can help them manage conflicts positively.

Materials:

one copy of the experience sheet, "Conflict Clipping," for each student; chart paper and marking pens

Note:

This is a two-part activity with a homework assignment in between.

Directions:

Distribute the experience sheet, "Conflict Clipping," and explain the homework assignment. In your own words say: *Your assignment is to find a newspaper or internet article, cartoon, or photograph depicting a conflict. Review the article, cartoon or photograph and answer the questions on the experience sheet. Bring both the clipping and the experience sheet to our next session.*

To ensure understanding, review the four types of conflict listed on the experience sheet. Use these questions to facilitate discussion:

— What kind of conflict are you having when you can't decide between two things that you want to buy?
— When one nation sends troops to attack another nation, what kind of conflict is that?
— Can you think of any intergroup conflicts that occur in our cities? ...our nation?
— Can you think of an international conflict that is happening right now or happened recently?

At the next session, ask the students to take out their homework assignment. Each student should have completed the experience sheet and brought in a current-events article, photograph or cartoon illustrating a conflict situation.

Have the students take turns summarizing their articles and sharing their responses from the completed experience sheet. The following questions may help focus the discussion:

— *Which type of conflict (of the four major types) is illustrated by your article (photograph, cartoon)? Explain the reasoning behind your selection.*
— *Which type of conflict seems to be most common? Why do you think that is?*
— *What seem to be common conflict words that come from your articles?*
— *Does anyone want to guess how the conflict in their article will be resolved?*

Next, ask the students to brainstorm words that seem to be related to conflict. Suggest that they try to recall words used in the various news articles. List their contributions on the board or chart paper.

Ask the students to look at the list and to identify those words that are most often associated with each of the four types of conflict. Indicate these associations by placing letters or symbols next to the words.

Finally, have the students review the list and see how many positive words they can find that are used to describe conflict. When they notice the overwhelming number of negative words, ask:

Do you think negative words are used to describe conflict because conflict itself is negative, or because most of the conflicts we hear and read about are poorly managed?

Remind the students that conflict is a process that can have good and bad results. Ask them which kind most news stories are about.

To conclude the activity, make a final list of positive words. Begin by transferring positive words from the news-story list; then brainstorm additional positive words related to well-managed conflict. For contrast, post this positive-word list next to the original negative-word list. Facilitate a culminating discussion.

Discussion Questions:

1. Why is it important to know what words, both positive and negative, are frequently associated with conflict?
2. If someone approaches you and starts using a lot of negative words concerning a conflict situation, what do you think? How do you feel?
3. If someone talked to you using a lot of aggressive words, what might happen if you used positive words to respond?
4. How can this information help you resolve conflict?

Conflict Clipping
Experience Sheet

Look in a recent newspaper, magazine or on the internet, and find a current events article, photograph, or cartoon about some kind of conflict. Print it or cut it out. Answer the questions below. Bring this sheet and the article, photo, or cartoon to the next session.

1. What is this conflict about?

2. What type of conflict is it? <u>Circle one:</u>
   - Intrapersonal: conflict within an individual
   - Interpersonal: conflict between two or more individuals
   - Intergroup: conflict between organizations or groups of people
   - International: conflict between nations or countries

3. Who is involved in the conflict?

4. What does each person (or group, or nation) want?

5. What do you think will happen?

How Conflict Escalates
Discussion and Drama

Objectives —

Students will:
— discover that conflicts can take on a life of their own and quickly escalate.
— become aware of the factors that trigger conflict and lead to its escalation.
— learn that conscious control of behaviors is the key to managing conflict.

Materials:

whiteboard; writing materials; one copy of the "Conflict Escalator Guide (SAMPLE)" and the blank "Conflict Escalator Guide" for each work group

Information to Share:

Conflicts tend to escalate if not managed. They can become unwieldy and even unmanageable if they move toward violent behavior. Conflicts can escalate quickly and need to be attended to immediately if negative outcomes and consequences are to be avoided. The simplest conflict management tool is just to be aware that you are in a conflict, so you can begin to take charge of it.

Directions:

Have students organize themselves into groups of five or six. Give each group a copy of the "Conflict Escalator Guide (SAMPLE)."

Introduce the activity by telling the students that they will be working in their small groups to create a conflict scenario. Referring to the "Conflict Escalator Guide (SAMPLE)," explain that each group, using a blank guide, will create a conflict scenario in which the conflict escalates as two people exchange statements and behaviors. Review the sample script with the students to illustrate your meaning. Point out that there will be five exchanges between Person A and Person B. Tell the students that they can substitute names for A and B. Note that behaviors as well as words contribute to conflict.

Provide each group with a blank copy of the "Conflict Escalator Guide." Suggest that the groups create a conflict between two friends, two members of a family, or between a student and a teacher (or other authority figure). Point out that the groups are to create a series of exchanges between these people and enter each statement and/or behavior in the appropriate place on the escalator chart beginning with Exchange #1 and working up the chart as the conflict escalates. **Important!** Be sure to caution the groups not to go to the point of violence. Allow time for the groups to create their scenarios.

Next, instruct the groups to prepare and practice a role play of their scenario. If you like, provide props. Encourage the students to have fun, over-dramatizing their role plays to heighten the effects.

After the groups have had sufficient time to practice, ask each one to present its role play to the class. **Important!** Make sure that each role play does indeed demonstrate escalation. If necessary, suggest appropriate changes.

Generate a discussion by asking the following questions:

Discussion Questions:

1. Did you notice the intensity of responses change as the conflict escalated? In what ways did it change?
2. Thinking about the role plays and your own conflicts, how do feelings change as conflicts escalate?

3. In what ways did the <u>focus</u> of the exchanges alter as the conflict escalated? (In most cases, they will have moved from an object to personal attacks.)

4. Have you ever wished, in retrospect, that you had handled a conflict differently? If so, how does your wish relate to staying in control during the conflict?
5. In what ways do our statements and behaviors in a conflict trigger escalation?
6. If the things we say and do in conflict have a lot to do with whether the conflict escalates, what is the most important thing a person can learn to do to keep conflicts from escalating and getting out of hand? (Find ways of staying in conscious control of language and behaviors; avoid reacting to the things others say and do, etc.)

Conflict Escalator Guide – SAMPLE

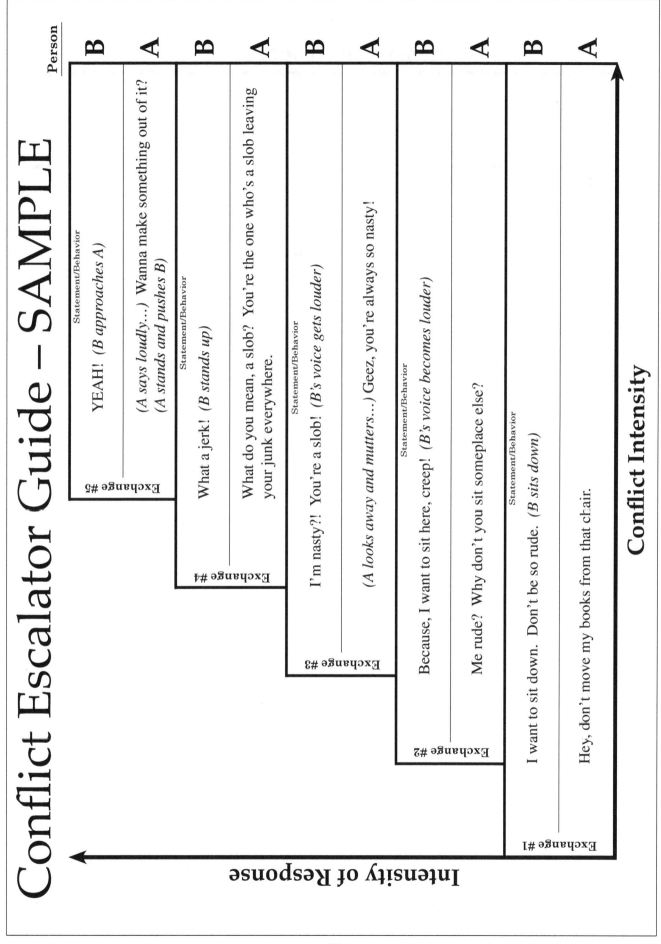

Person

Exchange #5

Statement/Behavior

B — YEAH! *(B approaches A)*

A — *(A says loudly...)* Wanna make something out of it? *(A stands and pushes B)*

Exchange #4

Statement/Behavior

B — What a jerk! *(B stands up)*

A — What do you mean, a slob? You're the one who's a slob leaving your junk everywhere.

Exchange #3

Statement/Behavior

B — I'm nasty?! You're a slob! *(B's voice gets louder)*

A — *(A looks away and mutters...)* Geez, you're always so nasty!

Exchange #2

Statement/Behavior

B — Because, I want to sit here, creep! *(B's voice becomes louder)*

A — Me rude? Why don't you sit someplace else?

Exchange #1

Statement/Behavior

B — I want to sit down. Don't be so rude. *(B sits down)*

A — Hey, don't move my books from that chair.

Conflict Intensity

Intensity of Response

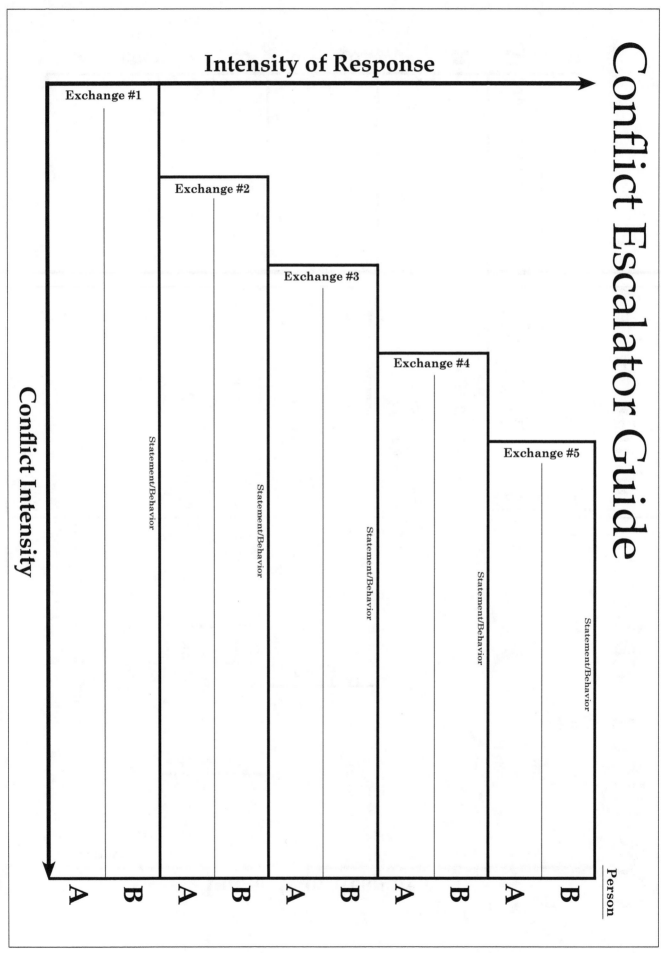

Conflict Escalator Guide

Intensity of Response

Conflict Intensity

Exchange #1

Exchange #2

Exchange #3

Exchange #4

Exchange #5

Statement/Behavior

Statement/Behavior

Statement/Behavior

Statement/Behavior

Statement/Behavior

A   B   A   B   A   B   A   B   A   B

Person

My Conflict Style
Group Discussion and Role Play

Objectives:

The students will:
— identify some of their characteristic conflict management styles.
— state the importance of consciously controlling their behaviors in conflict situations.
— differentiate between conflict styles and management strategies and approaches.

Materials:

whiteboard

Information to Share:

We all have characteristic ways in which we respond to conflicts. These are called our conflict styles. They have developed over time, and we use them because they seem to work. Very often, however, our styles don't work as well as other approaches might. We use our styles because they are automatic. Approaches we have to <u>think about</u> or <u>consider</u> are called strategies. Their use requires that we maintain conscious control of our behaviors during conflict and thoughtfully choose an approach we think will prove effective in successfully resolving the situation.

Directions:

To introduce this activity reproduce the following chart on the board:

STYLES	vs	APPROACHES OR STRATEGIES
Unconscious		Conscious
Automatic		Thoughtful/Purposeful
Reactive		Pro-active

Conduct a discussion about the differences between these terms. Emphasize that when we are using our styles we are probably not in conscious control of either ourselves or the situation.

Ask the students to form small groups of six to eight and arrange themselves around the room with plenty of space between groups.

To prepare for the rest of this activity tell the groups that they are to discuss the following topic: "A Time I Was in a Conflict and Could Have Handled It Better."

In your own words, explain the topic: *We are all regularly involved in conflicts of different types and proportions. Think of a conflict you experienced that you realized— after you had a chance to think about it later—could have been handled better. Perhaps you lost control and blew up; maybe you damaged a relationship or hurt someone's feelings. Take a moment and think of a time you wished you'd handled a conflict situation better. Remember the topic is, "A Time I Was in a Conflict and Could Have Handled It Better."*

Ask each member of the group to share for about 1-2 minutes concerning a single conflict. After the groups have finished sharing (allow about 15 minutes), generate a discussion by asking some or all of the following questions:

— *When we're in conflict with someone who is important to us, is it better to win or to save the relationship? ...Why?*
— *What is the difference between winning a conflict and resolving a conflict?*
— *To what extent did you feel in personal control during the conflict you shared?*

After this discussion, ask each group to review the conflicts that they shared and select one to role play. In your own words, give these instructions: *The person whose conflict is chosen should repeat what she or he shared with as much detail as possible so that everyone in the group has a clear picture of what happened. You may ask questions when you don't understand something. After retelling the story, the same student should select people to play various roles. That person should play him- or herself, and should also act as the director. It is the job of the director to make sure that the presentation fairly portrays the conflict. You will have 20 minutes to create and rehearse your role play. When presented to the rest of the class, it should be no more than 5 minutes in length. Make the role play enjoyable for yourselves and the rest of us.*

Caution: Tell the groups that if their chosen conflict involves violence, they must <u>stop</u> the role play short of the point where violence erupts.

When the groups are ready, have them act out their conflicts for the rest of the class.

Discussion Questions:

Immediately after the presentations, generate a class discussion with the following questions:

1. How would you have handled any of these conflicts differently? Can you see how your conflict style differs from the styles of others?
2. Do we generally think in a conflict situation, or do we merely react? What is the difference?
3. How do you feel when you manage to stay in conscious control of yourself and your behavior in a conflict?
4. (Referring to the chart on the board, ask...) What differences—besides those shown—can you think of between conflict styles and strategies?
5. How do you suppose we developed our styles for reacting to conflict?
6. What are some styles you have that you would like to replace with conscious approaches or strategies? (tendency to lose my temper, blow up, throw things, pout, withdraw, seek revenge, feel bad about myself, get defensive, etc.)
7. What are some of the most important things you've learned about conflict in this activity?
8. What questions would you like to ask me about conflict?

Assessing Anger Styles
Experience Sheet and Discussion

Objectives:

The students will:
— identify a recent event that caused them to feel angry and describe what they did.
— assess the effectiveness of their typical behaviors when angry.
— examine and discuss several common "anger styles."
— explain how they can choose more effective responses in situations that provoke anger.

Materials:

one copy of the experience sheet, "Assessing Your Anger" for each student; whiteboard

Information to Share:

Anger is a normal emotion. We all have characteristic ways of expressing anger. For purposes of this activity, these are called *anger styles*. Although anger styles are probably learned (as opposed to inborn), they are deeply ingrained and therefore automatic—almost like reflexes. The results our anger styles produce have reinforced our tendency to repeat them over the years. Still, they may not be the most effective or productive behaviors to use in every situation. Learning to consciously choose how we express our anger will help us become better managers of conflict.

Directions:

Write the word *anger* on the board. Ask the students what kind of feelings the word or subject causes them to experience. Listen to their responses, jotting notes on the board.

Explain that the class is going to discuss the subject of anger in some depth, but first you want the students to help by individually answering some questions.

Distribute the experience sheet, "Assessing Your Anger," and quickly go over the directions. Give the students time to fill out the sheet. Encourage quiet reflection.

Call time. Have the students choose partners and briefly share what they have written.

Convene the entire group and ask volunteers to tell the class what "style" they typically use to express their anger. Write their contributions on the board, generating a list of anger styles. Fill in with suggestions of your own until your list covers all of the styles listed on the next page (it may include more). Once a style is listed, acknowledge additional examples of that style by putting a check mark after the descriptor.

Anger Styles

- **Blowing up/attacking**
- **Withdrawing, refusing to talk**
- **Suppressing, denying, hiding feelings**
  — pretending, being phoney
  — use of alcohol and/or other drugs
  — overeating
  — excessive TV
- **Getting even**
  — in hidden ways (passive-aggressive)
  — openly, through punishment
- **Displacing feelings (taking them out on someone/something else)**
- **Releasing anger through stress-reduction**
  — exercise
  — tasks/chores that require physical activity
  — relaxation/music/meditation
  — talking with a friend, parent, counselor, etc.
- **Assertively confronting the situation**
  — explaining the problem and your feelings
  — attacking the problem, not the person.

Lead a discussion about how anger styles are developed and what purposes they serve (see "Information to Share"). Stress the need to decide when a style is productive and when it is not, and to consciously choose to respond in alternative ways when a style is not effective.

Conclude the activity by asking these and your own questions.

Discussion Questions:

1. How do we develop our styles of expressing anger?
2. Why do we persist in behaving in ways that don't work?
3. Why is anger such a difficult emotion to deal with?
4. Under what circumstances would it be best to use stress-reduction techniques to deal with your anger, rather than confront the other person?
5. What skills do you need to have in order to assertively confront a situation or person and try to solve the problem that caused your anger?

Extension:

Have the students do cost-benefit analyses of the major anger styles. Form groups of about six students, and assign each group a different style. Distribute chart paper and markers. Have a recorder in each group write the anger style as a heading across the top of a sheet. In two vertical columns, one labeled *Benefits* (+), the other labeled *Costs* (-), have the students brainstorm and list positive and negative outcomes, fallout, feelings, etc., that can occur as a result of using that style. Have the groups share their lists with the class. Discuss.

Assessing Your Anger
Experience Sheet

Try to remember a recent incident in which you became angry. Think carefully about what happened and answer these questions as honestly as you can.

What caused your anger?

How intense were your feelings?

Mildly Annoyed   **Furious**

How did your body feel?

What were your thoughts?

What *did* you feel like doing?

What did you do?

What was the result?

How effective was your behavior? Did it make matters a lot worse, or did it produce the results you wanted without hurting anyone? Explain:

Reading Body Language
Experience Sheet, Role Play, and Discussion

Objectives:

The students will:
— identify components of "body language."
— describe and demonstrate incidents in which the body language of a person did not match the person's spoken language.
— discuss the possible effects of contradictory body language, particularly as it relates to conflict.

Materials:

one copy of the experience sheet, "What Is Your Body Saying?" for each student; whiteboard

Information to Share:

The way we use our bodies to communicate is very deeply ingrained. We signal each other, using various nonverbal cues, most of which are learned but some of which are probably innate (the same for humans everywhere). Our *body language* usually projects the same message as our words, emphasizing and punctuating what we say. But this is not always the case. If we are lying, or pretending, or being phoney, our body language will tend to contradict our words. Which do we believe? Studies have shown that most people trust body language more than they trust words. In conflict management, it is important to realize that we show attitudes such as liking or disliking not by what we actually say, but by the way we say it and the expressions that accompany our speech.

Directions:

Begin this activity by posing a series of evocative questions, such as:

— *Have you ever strongly sensed that a friend was annoyed or troubled, and asked, "Is something wrong?" only to have that person answer, "No, I'm okay"?*
— *Have you ever asked, "How are you?" and received the usual "Fine," but concluded to yourself that the person was definitely <u>not fine</u>?*
— *What were you responding to in cases like these?*

The students will probably say that they could tell by the way the person "acted" that something was wrong. Encourage them to describe specifically what kinds of cues they were responding to and write these on the board. Continue to give additional examples (or elicit them from the class) until you have a fairly complete list of elements that comprise "body language."

Facial expression
Eye contact
Use of voice
Posture
Gesture
Distance
Touch

Next, ask the students to form groups of six to eight. Write the following topic on the board:

"A Time Someone's Actions Spoke Louder Than Words"

Tell the students that you want them to take turns sharing a real experience in which they "listened" to someone's body language and it contradicted what the person was saying. Suggest that they briefly describe the incident, what they thought was really going on, and how they responded. (Note: If your students have started participating in Sharing Circles, have them adhere to the Sharing Circle session procedures and rules.)

When the groups have finished sharing, instruct them to select one example from the incidents that were shared and act it out for the rest of the class. Urge them to choose an example in which spoken language and body language were clearly contradictory, and to role play not only the initial exchange between the two people, but what happened as a result. Give the groups a few minutes to make their selections and rehearse.

After each role play, talk with the players and the class about what was really going on in the situation. Then direct the players to repeat the scene, showing what might have happened if the person's words had matched his or her body language. Coach, as necessary.

Distribute the experience sheet, "What Is Your Body Saying?" and give the students a few minutes to read it. Using information from the experience sheet, as well as from "Information to Share" (above), lead a culminating discussion.

Discussion Questions:

1. How do you feel when someone denies a feeling or problem that you are quite certain exists?
2. How does body language—e.g., a hostile expression or a "cold shoulder"—contribute to conflict?
3. If you were trying to resolve a conflict with someone, what would you look for in that person's body language? What would make you feel guarded or suspicious? What would build trust?

What Is Your Body Saying?
Experience Sheet

No matter what you say in words, people are probably "listening" just as much or more to your body language. Good communicators make sure that their facial expressions, voice, posture, and gestures send the same messages as their words. Good communicators also learn to pay attention to the body language of others.

Facial Expression

Keep in mind that your face—particularly your eyes, eyebrows, forehead and mouth—are dead giveaways to your emotions. For example, blank looks may cause people to think you are either angry or not interested. A weak smile that fades quickly suggests that you are not sincere.

Eye Contact

Look at the other person a lot, but don't stare. Eye contact shows that you are listening and interested; glancing away from time to time provides both you and the other person a relaxing break. Avoiding eye contact may show that you are nervous or lack confidence. Staring may cause you to look angry or threatening.

Use of Voice

Most of the time, it is appropriate to speak in a moderate volume, varying tone, pitch, and pace to fit what you are saying. A loud or booming tone may sound threatening. A low volume, thin tone, or extremely slow pace may show weakness, lack of confidence, or depression.

Posture

If you want to look attentive, lean forward with a straight back and with you arms in an open position (not folded across your chest or clasped behind your back). Turn toward the other person. If you want to appear relaxed, lean back, but keep your head up. Avoid slumped shoulders, bowed head, folded arms and caved-in chest. Do not turn your body away. These cues convey weakness, depression and lack of interest.

Gestures

Use gestures to emphasize what you say, making your words livelier and easier to understand. Also use gestures to clarify meaning. Be aware of small movements that tend to say a lot. For example, fidgeting may show anxiety; foot-tapping may show irritation; playing with hair or clothing suggest boredom.

Distance

Keep an appropriate distance between you and the other people you are with. Standing too close may make a person feel uncomfortable—even threatened. Turning away or creating too much distance gives the impression that you are cold or uninterested.

Touch

A brief touch on the hand, arm, or shoulder can convey warmth and emotional support. If a person tenses or draws away, that person probably doesn't want to be touched at all. Respect those signals. Avoid sudden, rough touches, and never touch unacceptable parts of a person's body.

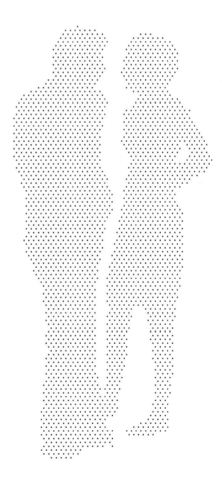

Mastering Assertive Communication
Experience Sheet, Role Play, and Discussion

Objectives:

The students will:
— describe the differences between assertive, aggressive, and passive behaviors.
— practice assertive and non-assertive behaviors in role play situations.
— explain how assertive, aggressive, and passive behaviors affect conflict situations.

Materials:

one copy of the experience sheet, "Reacting Assertively," for each student

Information to Share:

We all have a choice whether we communicate passively, aggressively, or assertively. Sometimes people act passively or aggressively because they haven't learned how to be assertive. When this is the case, it is difficult for people to get their needs met or their ideas expressed.

Directions:

Ask the students: "Have you ever felt taken advantage of or misunderstood? Do you think this might have happened because you weren't assertive?"

Distribute the experience sheets. Read the definitions of Aggressive, Passive, and Assertive together. Discuss the differences. Give some examples from your own experience. Have the students pair up, and test their ability to discriminate between the three types of responses by completing the remainder of the experience sheet. Go over the answers in the larger group. Invite some of the dyad pairs to role play the different situations. Have them role play

all three responses, and then discuss the differences between the three. Facilitate discussion throughout the role plays.

Discussion Questions:

1. How did you feel when you were being aggressive? ...passive? ...assertive?
2. How did you feel when you were on the receiving end of an aggressive response? ...a passive response? ...an assertive response?
3. How do you react when someone almost always responds aggressively, but disguises his or her responses with humor?
4. What causes people to respond passively?
5. How is a conflict situation affected when one person is very passive? ...very aggressive?
6. How does being assertive help people resolve conflicts?
7. What skills do you need to practice in order to become comfortably assertive?

Reacting Assertively
Experience Sheet

What does it mean to be aggressive, passive, or assertive?

People are aggressive when they:
- intentionally attack, take advantage of, humiliate, hurt, or put down others.
- act on the belief that others are not as important as they are.

The aggressive person's mottos are:
"Get them before they get you."
"How you play doesn't count, only that you win."
"Never give a sucker an even break."

People are passive when they:
- invite, encourage, or permit others to take advantage of them.
- discount themselves and act as if others are more important than they are.

The passive person's mottos are:
"I should never make anyone feel uncomfortable, resentful, or displeased, except myself."
"I should never give anyone a headache or stomachache, except myself."
"I should never disappoint anyone or cause anyone to disapprove of me."

People are assertive when they:
- express themselves openly and honestly to communicate their needs, wants, or feelings, without demanding or discounting the wants, needs, or feelings of others.
- act according to the belief that all people including themselves are equally important.

The assertive person's mottos are:
"I have the right to ask for anything I want."
"If I want something and don't ask for it, I forfeit my right to complain."
"Others have an equal right to ask for what they want."
"I recognize their rights without discounting my own."

Decide which of the following responses are passive, aggressive, and assertive. In the space in front of each response put either a "P" for passive, "AG" for aggressive, or "AS" for assertive.

• Ms. Reynolds, Tyrone's history teacher, tells Tyrone that his homework is unacceptable, and he must redo it to get a grade. Tyrone replies:

____ "I'm so stupid. I never get anything right."

____ "No way! That's totally unfair!"

____ "I'll do the homework over, Ms. Reynolds, but I need to talk to you first, so that I'll get it right this time."

• Tony asks Nushene to go to the dance with him. Ross gets mad when he finds out, because he asked Nushene, too. Ross tells Tony to back off. Tony replies:

____ "Tough! She wouldn't go with a jerk like you, anyway!"

____ "Sure, Ross. Gosh, I'm awful sorry, really."

____ "I think I have the right to ask Linda if I want to."

• Lydia asks her friend Alice to help her carry some things to the auditorium. Alice responds:

____ "I'm going to be late for English, but if you want me to, okay."

____ "What's the matter with you? Are your arms broken?"

____ "I can't help you right now, Lydia. I have to get to my English class."

• Ashley realizes, upon leaving the supermarket, that she has been short-changed 65 cents. She returns, but the cashier denies the mistake. Ashley says:

____ "You're a liar. Give me my 65 cents right now!"

____ "Well, um, I guess I must have miscounted. Sorry to bother you."

____ "I'm sure about this. Here, count the change yourself."

• Andy returns a pair of jeans to the store because the zipper is broken. The clerk says:

___ "Yes, that's a broken zipper all right. Can I get you another pair?"

___ "Oh, I'm so sorry. I should have checked the jeans before I sold them to you. It's all my fault."

___ "You broke this zipper didn't you? Well, you're not going to cheat us!"

• David's parents have outlined some chores for him to do around the house and yard, but he's fallen behind. His dad threatens to ground David if he doesn't meet his responsibilities before the week-end. David says:

___ "I guess I'm just a worthless slob."

___ "You're trying to make my life miserable. This is abuse. You'll be sorry!"

___ "I've been concerned about the chores, too. I'll rearrange my schedule and get them done."

• Natalie drives into the parking lot of a small mall, but all the handicapped spaces are taken, so she has to park in a regular spot and then struggle to remove her chair from the back seat. As she's passing one of the handicapped spaces, Natalie almost collides with a young man running to his car. She says:

___ "Thanks to you, Mister, I just had to struggle for 20 minutes getting out of my car. Maybe when you have to pay a fine, you'll stop be-ing so selfish."

___ "Hi. I guess maybe you didn't notice that's a handicapped spot?"

___ "You violate my rights when you take a spot that's reserved for people with disabilities. I hope you won't do it again."

• When she comes home from work, Omar's mother brings his bike in out of the rain. When Omar thanks her, she says:

___ "Oh, don't thank me. I'm gone so much of the time, I should thank you for even being here."

___ "If you weren't such a moron, you wouldn't have left it out in the rain in the first place."

___ "I'm glad I could help you."

Passive Aggressive or Assertive?

Developing Conflict Resolution Skills

Students need to become acquainted with a range of conflict management strategies, discussing the relative pros and cons of each. In addition, they need many opportunities to practice conflict management strategies safely and enjoyably, so that they can internalize and refine their skills.

This section includes specific strategies that help students handle both unexpected and planned confrontations, resolve conflicts, cope with and reduce anger, manage the residual feelings that follow conflict, and openly receive and evaluate criticism.

In addition to the role plays and other practice techniques imbedded in the activities, several additional approaches to behavioral rehearsal are outlined, including role-play variations, and the use of reading, writing, and art assignments — all appropriate for secondary classrooms and counseling groups. Finally, a number of role-play starters are provided in the form of conflict scenarios typical of those encountered by young people.

Rules for A Fair Fight
Imagery, Discussion, and Small-Group Brainstorming

Objectives:

The students will:
— describe the similarities between a conflict and a game or sport.
— develop rules intended to ensure that conflicts are handled fairly.

Materials:

chart paper and markers for each work group; masking tape; whiteboard

Information to Share:

Conflict is normal. While most of us don't go out the door each morning looking for conflicts, we tend to encounter one or two just about every day. If we think of conflict as a contest—like a tennis match or a game of volleyball—we recognize that it is a *cooperative event*, a challenge, a test of skills. If we really want to perform well on the conflict court, we have to know the rules of the sport, avoid making too many fouls, present ourselves and our ideas in the most effective ways possible, and respect the rights of our opponent. We have to fight fair. Guidelines for fighting fair might include:

- Identify and focus on the problem.
- Attack the problem, not the person.
- Listen to your opponent.
- Demonstrate respect.
- Take responsibility for your own actions.

Directions:

Ask the students to think of a sport or game they enjoy playing—baseball, chess, tennis, volleyball, wrestling, basketball, Monopoly, Scrabble, etc. Tell them to take a few moments, close their eyes, and imagine themselves playing that game with a skilled opponent, being totally involved and energized.

Now, without opening their eyes, ask the students to recall a recent conflict they had with another person—anything from a mild disagreement to a noisy fight. Tell them to picture this contest in as much detail as possible.

Next, suggest that the students allow their minds to transform that image of conflict into a sport or game, seeing it as a contest of opposing ideas, opinions, beliefs, perceptions—whatever it actually was. The opponents in the conflict may not agree, but the fact that they are interacting means that they are playing this game *cooperatively*.

Invite the students to open their eyes and comment on this imagery experience. Generate a discussion about the analogy of conflict as game or sport. Encourage the students to further develop the notion, while making key points of your own (see "Information to Share")

On the board, write this heading:

RULES FOR A FAIR FIGHT

Ask the students to form work groups of five to eight, and choose a recorder. Distribute the chart paper and markers.

Tell the groups that you want them to brainstorm a list of rules for the game of conflict. In your own words say to them: *Your list doesn't have to be long, but it should accomplish certain things. Rules ensure an even start, safety, and adherence to certain agreed-upon behaviors throughout the game. Rules protect both the players and the object of the game. It may help to think about the rules of a specific sport or game and keep those in mind as you work.*

Allow 10-15 minutes for brainstorming. Then have the groups display their lists and share them with the class. Facilitate a culminating discussion.

Discussion Questions:

1. What are some of the benefits of thinking of conflict as a game with rules?
2. When you are in a conflict, how can you encourage the other person to "fight fair."
3. What can you say or do when the other person keeps breaking the rules?
4. What have you learned about conflict from this exercise?

Extension:

If time permits, have the groups brainstorm a second list—a list of GAME FOULS. Explain that, just as in a sport, fouls are behaviors that are not allowed because they create an unfair advantage, are disrespectful or dangerous, or destroy the object of the game. Have the groups display and explain their two lists, side-by-side.

Exploring Alternatives to Conflict
Dramatizations and Discussion

Objectives:

The students will
— learn and practice specific strategies for resolving conflict.

Materials:

a copy of one scenario (from the list on the next two pages) for each group of students; one copy of the experience sheet, "Conflict Resolution Strategies," for each student

Directions:

Distribute the experience sheet entitled, "Conflict Resolution Strategies," to each student.

On the board, write the heading "Strategies for Resolving Conflict." Explain to the students that in conflict situations, certain kinds of behaviors tend to help people solve their problems. List the strategies shown below, while the students follow along on their experience sheets. Give examples, and ask the students to describe problems that might be resolved by each alternative.

- **Sharing:** Using/doing something with another person.
- **Taking turns:** Alternately using/ doing something with another person.
- **Active Listening:** Hearing the other person's feelings or opinions.
- **Postponing:** Deciding to put off dealing with the conflict until another time.
- **Using humor:** Looking at the situation in a comical way; making light of the situation but not the person.

- **Compromising:** Giving up part, in order to get the remainder, of what one wants.
- **Expressing regret:** Saying that you are sorry about the situation, without taking the blame if it's not your fault.
- **Problem solving:** Discussing the problem; trying to find a mutually acceptable solution.

Divide the class into small groups and give each group a conflict scenario (from the next two pages). Instruct the groups to discuss the scenario and pick a conflict management strategy from the list of alternatives on the board. Have each group practice the scenarios and then act out the conflict and its resolution, while the rest of the class tries to guess which alternative they are using. At the conclusion of the role plays, lead a class discussion.

Discussion Questions:

1. Why is it better to practice positive alternatives, rather than wait for a conflict to occur and then try them?
2. Which strategies are hardest to use and why? Which are easiest? Which work best and why?
3. At what point do you think you should get help to resolve a conflict?

Conflict Scenarios

Scenario 1:

Your group is working on an economics project. You are using the computer to develop a series of charts showing the operations of the Federal Reserve System. As a final step, you plan to use a graphics program to draw illustrations for the charts. However, another group member also wants to do the illustrations. The two of you start arguing about who should get the job and other group members take sides. The situation becomes very tense and noisy and the project is in danger of being ruined. Your teacher approaches the group and warns you to solve the problem—or forget the project.

Scenario 2:

You plan to go to the movies on Saturday afternoon with a friend. Your family suddenly decides to hold a yard clean-up on Saturday, and this makes you very upset. You start to argue with your parents, insisting that since you have done your homework and chores all week, you deserve to spend Saturday afternoon at the movie. Besides, your friend's parents have agreed to let the two of you use their car. You are in danger of being put on restriction because you are starting to yell at your parents.

Scenario 3:

Without realizing it, you dropped (and lost) your homework on the way to school. That has put you in a bad mood. In gym, a classmate accidently hits you in the back with a soccer ball. You react in anger and threaten to beat up your classmate after school. This makes the classmate angry and he or she reluctantly agrees to fight. Other classmates take sides and are talking about staying after school to watch the fight. During lunch, you have a chance to think about it. Your realize that you picked the fight because you were upset about your lost homework. You didn't like being hit by the ball, but think that maybe it isn't worth a fight.

Scenario 4:

You make plans with a few friends to meet a half hour before school to play a quick game of basketball. You get up early, but decide to watch TV instead of meeting your friends. When you get to school, your friends are angry. They say you messed up the game by making one of the teams a person short. They want you to know that you let them down. Before they can express their feelings, you start making excuses. You don't give them a chance to talk. They start to walk away.

Scenario 5:

Two students share a locker at school. One of the students is in a rush one day and unknowingly leaves the locker open. When the second student discovers the open locker an hour later, a jacket and a CD are missing. The second student blames the first, who denies responsibility. They start to fight.

Conflict Resolution Strategies

Have you ever been in a conflict? Of course! No matter how much you try to avoid them, conflicts happen. They are part of life. What makes conflicts upsetting is not knowing how to handle them. If you don't know something helpful to do, you may end up making things worse. So study these strategies, and the next time you see a conflict coming, try one!

1. Share.
Whatever the conflict is about, keep (or use) some of it yourself, and let the other person have or use some.

5. Use humor.
Look at the situation in a comical way. Don't take it too seriously. Be sure you're laughing at the situation and not the person.

2. Take turns.
Use or do something for a little while. Then let the other person take a turn.

I'll go to the park today, if you'll go to the movies tomorrow.

OK — I can agree to that.

6. Compromise.
Offer to give up part of what you want and ask the other person to do the same.

3. Active Listen.
Let the other person talk while you listen carefully. Really try to understand the person's feelings and ideas.

7. Express regret.
Say that you are sorry about the situation, *without* taking the blame if it's not your fault. If it is your fault, admit it.

4. Postpone.
If you or the other person are very angry or tired, put off dealing with the conflict until another time.

How we can solve our problem:

8. Problem solve.
Discuss the problem and try to find a solution that is acceptable to both you and the other person.

Problem Solving:
The Win-Win Strategy
Experience Sheet and Discussion

Objectives:

The students will:
— examine a win-win problem solving process and discuss its benefits.
— practice using problem solving to resolve specific conflicts.

Materials:

one copy of the experience sheet, "Getting to Win-Win" for each student; copies of "Conflict Scenarios" (page 111) for optional use during skill practice; whiteboard

Note: This activity works best if it is carried out following the activity, "Exploring Alternatives to Conflict."

Information to Share:

Of all the strategies for resolving conflicts, problem solving is the most productive—the one most likely to leave both parties feeling satisfied. By working together to develop the best possible solution, disputants:

• interact in positive ways.
• listen to each other's concerns.
• combine their brain power to create alternative solutions.
• choose a solution that allows both to feel they have "won."

Directions:

Begin by reviewing the various strategies for resolving conflict presented in the activity, "Exploring Alternatives to Conflict." Explain that the final strategy — problem solving — is particularly desirable

because it promotes positive interaction between the parties to the conflict, and because both people "win." However, problem solving is also more involved and takes more time.

Distribute copies of the experience sheet and give the students a few minutes to read it. Ask for questions and facilitate a discussion of the benefits of the process outlined (see "Information to Share").

Have the students get together in pairs to practice the win-win process. Distribute copies of the "Conflict Scenarios." Tell the students they may use either a fictional conflict from the sheet or a real conflict from their own experience. They are to work together to develop a win-win resolution to their conflict scenarios.

Circulate and monitor the progress of the pairs. Answer questions and provide coaching, as necessary. When most pairs seem to have completed the problem-solving process, facilitate a discussion.

If time permits, have the students change partners and complete a second round of practice.

Discussion Questions:

1. How did you feel as you worked together to resolve your conflict?
2. How satisfied are you with your solution? Explain.
3. What are the hardest parts of the process? ...the easiest parts?
4. Problem solving doesn't work for every conflict. When do you think you would use this strategy? For what kinds of conflicts do you think problem solving would be ineffective or inappropriate?
5. What skills do you need to work on in order to improve your ability to handle conflict this way?

Getting to Win-Win
Experience Sheet

Have you ever had a conflict with one of your friends? If so, you know how easily conflict can damage a relationship. Sometimes it takes a long time to patch things up.

Here's a way of handling conflict that can actually make a relationship stronger. By following these steps, you can make sure that both you and your friend end up feeling pretty good. Try it!

When you are in a conflict:

1. Express your feelings and concerns in a positive, non-blaming fashion. An I-message is a good way to do this.

2. Try to use a calm tone of voice and open, attentive body language.

3. Listen actively to the other person's side of the story. Don't interrupt. Try to understand his or her perceptions and feelings.

4. If you don't understand something, ask for more information. Say, "Could you tell me more about that..." or "I don't think I understand. What exactly do you mean?"

5. Define the problem. After you have listened to each other's side of the story, work together to agree on exactly what the problem is. Include all parts of the problem in your definition.

6. Brainstorm possible solutions. You might want to write these down. Include all kinds of ideas, even ones that sound a little crazy.

7. Together, agree on the solution that has the best chance of solving the problem (the one you defined together). Combine several alternatives if necessary.

8. If no solution seems possible, put the problem on hold for a few days. Agree on a day and time to get together again. In the meantime, re-think the problem.

First Feelings
Looking at Anger as a Secondary Emotion

Objectives:

The students will:
— identify feelings that typically precede/precipitate anger and identify ways to deal with those feelings.
— practice acceptable ways to express "first feelings."

Materials:

one copy of the experience sheet, "Dealing with Anger," for each student; whiteboard

Directions:

Introduce this activity by explaining that anger is a normal emotion, experienced by everyone. However, anger tends to be a secondary emotion. In other words, one or more *other* feelings usually precede anger. These can be referred to as "first feelings." Give the students an example, such as: *You forget to study for a test and failed it. Because the test covered a subject in which you usually do well, you feel disappointed and frustrated. However, those "first feelings" quickly turn to anger. Before you know it, anger is the only feeling that you are aware of and the only one other people observe in you.*

Continue by introducing this second and related concept: Other people usually have difficulty coping with our anger. If our behavior becomes volatile and aggressive when we are angry, we cause others to feel threatened and maybe even to get angry in return. Other people have an easier time responding to our initial feeling of disappointment, frustration, embarrassment, grief, or fear. Consequently, a valuable skill to develop is the skill of identifying and expressing our initial feelings, rather than just our anger. Recognizing these first feelings is vital, which again reinforces the need to buy time in conflict situations.

Brainstorm some initial emotions that often precede anger and write them on the board. They can include feelings such as sadness, grief, frustration, embarrassment, relief, shock, disappointment, and confusion. Then ask the students to suggest acceptable ways of expressing these feelings that others can identify with.

Distribute the experience sheet, "Dealing with Anger." Explain to the students that they will read several scenarios in which anger is preceded by other emotions. Their task is to identify the "other emotions" and suggest ways in which they can be appropriately expressed. Read and discuss the first scenario together as guided practice. If you feel that the students have a good understanding of the concepts, allow them to do the rest of the experience sheet individually, in pairs, or in small groups.

Discussion Questions:

When the students have finished the sheet, gather the whole group together to discuss the other scenarios. Summarize this activity with a few thinking questions such as these:

1. How does anger mask what is really going on inside someone?
2. Why is anger so difficult to deal with in other people?
3. What are some initial feelings that often precede anger?
4. What are some ways in which we can express our "First Feelings"?

Dealing with Anger
Experience Sheet

Read the following scenarios carefully and answer the questions.

Scenario 1:

Maria was one of the best players on the hockey team. She really wanted to be captain the coming semester and had more than just a good chance of being elected. Her teammates liked and respected her and she got along well with her coach. Maria knew that her grades had to stay above a C and she struggled to keep her English grade up. Poor reading skills kept her from doing very well. When she took her final English test before semester's end, she thought she had done okay. When report cards came out, however, she saw a "D" in English. During hockey practice after school, Maria announced that she didn't want to be captain of the team. When her friends asked her why she had changed her mind, Maria snapped at them and said, "Who wants to be captain of this stupid team, anyway? I have better things to worry about than keeping you all in line."

Questions:

—What were Maria's initial feelings? _____

_____

_____

—How did she express these feelings? _____

_____

_____

—How could Maria have better expressed her emotions?

_____

_____

_____

Scenario 2:

Nate came to school ready for a fight. The night before, he lost his part time job and he really was counting on the money. Nate's friend, James, greeted him with a friendly punch, "What's up, Dude?" Nate didn't respond. He just fumed. James punched him a little harder and said, "What's the matter? You too good for me today?" At that, Nate went ballistic and started screaming at James, "Can't you keep your hands to yourself? You think you own the place!"

Questions:

—What were Nate's first feelings before he lost his temper?

_____

_____

—How did he express his emotions? _____

_____

—How could he have expressed his first feelings? _____

_____

_____

Scenario 3:

Marianne really wanted to be noticed by Mark. She was hoping that he would ask our to a special party that was coming up. Instead, Mark asked Marianne's best friend, Rachel. Marianne felt terrible. The next time Marianne saw Rachel she didn't want to talk to her, but Rachel came up and cheerily said, "Hi." Marianne responded by saying, "How could you do this to me. You know that I wanted to go to the party with Mark. You're really some friend!"

Questions:

—What were Marianne's first feelings when she found out Mark had asked Rachel?

_____

_____

—How did she express her emotions? _____

_____

—How could she have expressed her first feelings? _____

_____

_____

Taking Charge of Personal Anger

Dyad and Large Group Discussion

Objectives:

The students will:
— describe how they typically react when they are angry.
— examine a simple process for managing anger.
— discuss the importance of "buying time" when they are angry.

Materials:

whiteboard

Note: This activity and the one that follows should be done in sequence. They may be done in one class period (if time permits) or in two successive sessions.

Information to share:

- Anger is the by-product of almost every conflict.
- Conflict situations arise, and as we think about what's going on, we generate feelings of anger.
- When we feel angry, our bodies are charged with chemicals that give us negative feelings. By buying some time (it actually takes longer than just counting to ten) we allow these chemicals to dissipate and our feelings of anger begin to go away.

- Understanding that anger is the result of our thoughts gives us the opportunity to moderate anger by taking conscious control of the thoughts that precede it.
- When anger goes unmanaged, it can add fuel to a conflict and cause it to escalate. As one negative thought leads to another, anger increases and the conflict grows in size.
- Our anger can infect others, making them angry.
- The secret to avoiding or reversing this process lies in what we decide to do with our very first thoughts.

Directions:

Prior to class, write the following Anger Management Recipe on the board:

ANGER MANAGEMENT RECIPE

1. BUY YOURSELF SOME TIME!!!!!

2. Ask Yourself These Questions:

- Is this situation in any way similar to an experience from my past?

- How important is my relationship with this person? . . . What's my level of commitment?

- What other things are going on in my life?

- What's at risk in this situation?

Introduce the activity by asking: *How many of you have heard that the best thing to do when you are angry is to count to ten? Where do you suppose that idea came from?*

Facilitate student input, jotting ideas on the board. Briefly elaborate at appropriate points, referring to the "Anger Management Recipe" on the board and incorporating ideas from "Information to Share." Concepts to cover include:

- Counting to ten gives us time to calm down and gain control.
- Sometimes we react to the current situation because it reminds us of one from our past that didn't go well. It's like a *reflex*—probably a defensive one.

- The relative importance of the relationship often determines how much effort we're willing to put into resolving a conflict.
- Unrelated events or conditions in our lives may cause us to overreact emotionally and/or distort the importance of the conflict. Sometimes we *displace* feelings from one situation to another.
- The more at stake in a conflict, the more care we need to take obtaining a good resolution.

Have the students form pairs. Tell them to take 2 minutes each to describe the <u>very first</u> thing they typically do when they feel angry. (Signal the students when it is time to change speakers.)

After the students have shared in their pairs, reconvene the entire group and ask the students to call out the behaviors they described to their partners while you list them on the board. When you have finished, point to the list and ask:

— *When you respond this way, do you think about it first, or is your reaction automatic?*

— *If it's automatic (a <u>style</u> of responding), how can you make your first response more reasoned (a <u>strategy</u>)?*

Clarify that TIME is what is usually needed in order to choose an effective strategy instead of simply reacting. Go back to the recipe on the board and review the main concepts. Facilitate a culminating discussion.

Discussion Questions:

1. In what ways can the Anger Management Recipe help you?
2. What is the hardest thing about following this recipe?
3. Why is it difficult to stay in control when we are angry?
4. What is the most important ingredient in the recipe? Explain.

Extension:

Have the students participate in a second dyad in which they describe to their partner what they typically do when anger is directed at them.

Controlling Angry Thoughts
Small Group Activity and Discussion

Objectives:

The students will:
— show how a conflict event produces thoughts related to the event, which in turn produce feelings (often anger).
— state that a key to managing anger is buying time to think.
— practice substituting moderate thoughts for angry thoughts as one way of reducing anger.

Materials:

whiteboard; writing materials

Information to share:

Buying time allows us to gain control of and *moderate* our thoughts, which often reduces anger. This is because angry feelings are not actually caused by situations and events, but rather by the *thoughts* we have about those situations and events. Once the thoughts about an event (often extreme) are identified, those thoughts can be replaced with different thoughts (usually more moderate) as one way of controlling anger.

Directions:

Review the "Anger Management Recipe" from the previous activity with the students. Explain that you are going to demonstrate how buying time allows a person the opportunity to change his or her thoughts about a situation, which in turn can reduce anger.

Write four headings across the top of the board: **Event**, **Thoughts**, **Feelings**, and **Substitute Thoughts**. Under the **Event** column write *Mom won't let me go to the dance with my friends*. Skip the second column and ask the students what

their feelings might be in this situation. The students will probably suggest words such as mad, furious, and miserable. Write several of these words in the **Feelings** column. Then go back to the **Thoughts** column, and ask the students what their thoughts might be concerning the same situation. Elicit answers such as these: She's being mean or unreasonable. *She doesn't understand how important it is to me. She never wants me to have fun.*

Explain to the students that it is not the event, but the *thoughts* about the event that cause the feelings. Refer to the sentences in the second column and point out that any of these thoughts about the event could create angry feelings. Explain that no situation, event, or person *makes* us have a particular feeling. Through our thoughts, we *choose* our feelings, even if we are not aware of it.

Next, suggest that if the thoughts recorded in the second column can be moderated, the feelings too will change. Help the students create new thought statements such as: *Mom thinks she is looking out for my safety. She has family plans the night of the dance and wants me to be with the family. There will be more dances this year.* Record them in the last column, **Substitute Thoughts**. Point out that these moderated thoughts will reduce the anger.

Distribute writing materials, as necessary. Ask the students to divide a sheet of paper in half lengthwise creating two columns. Have them write the heading **Event** at the top of the left-hand column and the heading *Thoughts* at the top of the right-hand column. Next, instruct the students to turn their paper over and create two more columns. Direct them to write the headings *Feelings* and *Substitute Thoughts* above the left and right columns on this side.

Under the first heading, ask the students to list three real or hypothetical situations/events in which they are certain they would feel angry. In the second column (adjacent to each description), have them write the thoughts they would have in each situation. On the other side of the paper, ask them to write down the feelings that these thoughts would create. Finally, challenge the students to come up with moderated or more positive thoughts that could be substituted for the original thoughts about the situation.

When all of the students have completed their charts, invite individuals to share one or more of their "anger sequences." After each example, ask the group how their feelings might change as a result of the substitute thoughts. Emphasize that when they find themselves reacting to a situation too strongly, they can improve the situation and their disposition by rethinking the situation. To do this, they need to buy time. Both abilities takes practice and perseverance, but they work!

Discussion Questions:

To summarize, ask the students to think about and/or respond to the following questions:

1. Why do we choose to feel angry in certain situations?
2. When you are angry, why is it important to "buy yourself some time" to rethink the situation?
3. What is the benefit of substituting angry thoughts with positive thoughts?
4. What is easy about substituting angry thoughts with more positive thoughts? What is difficult about it?
5. What can you do to become skilled at substituting your angry thoughts?

Understanding and Managing Confrontations
Role Play and Discussion

Objectives:

The students will:
— explain the relationship between confrontations and conflict.
— differentiate between confrontations they initiate and those that are thrust upon them.
— demonstrate the use of active listening and I-messages in dealing with confrontations.

Materials:

whiteboard

Note: This activity uses skills and understandings that have been developed in previous activities, particularly "The Active Listener" and "How to Give An I-Message!"

Information to share:

- Many conflicts start with a confrontation between the people involved. Most people think of confrontation, like conflict, in negative terms.
- Three types of confrontations are:
  — *surprise* confrontation — the one we don't see coming
  — *spontaneous* confrontation — produced when something simple escalates into conflict.
  — *planned* confrontation—the one we initiate in order to turn a conflict into a manageable problem.
- Three skills which help limit the build-up of negative energy that often develops during confrontations are:
  — buying time
  — active listening
  — I-messages.

Directions:

Write the words conflict and confrontation on the board, and ask the students to help you define them. Record all contributions; through discussion, attempt to arrive at definitions that distinguish the two. For example:

Conflict: *a struggle or contest between people with opposing needs, ideas, beliefs or goals.*

Confrontation: *a face-to-face encounter or clash involving conflicting ideas or goals.*

Explain to the students that a confrontation is a specific, pivotal event in a conflict. Some conflicts start with a confrontation. In other cases, a conflict may be brewing for some time before a confrontation puts it on the table and forces the people involved to deal with it.

Regardless of when they occur, confrontations give us an opportunity to clear the air, define the problem, take charge, and start working on a solution.

The most effective skills to use during a confrontation are:

- active listening — when the other person confronts you
- I-messages *followed* by active listening — when you are doing the confronting.

Ask two volunteers who have a flair for the dramatic to come to the front of the class and help you with a role play. Ask volunteer #1 to angrily accuse #2 of forgetting to meet him or her after school as planned. Direct #2 to actively listen to what's being said and to feed back both the person's words and feelings. For example:

You've been waiting a long time for me, and you're pretty angry.

Allow the role play to continue through one or two additional exchanges. Then ask #2 if she or he can figure out what #1's "first feelings" (before the anger) might have been and feed those back. For example:

...Sounds like you got pretty tired standing around waiting for me.

OR

...You were afraid you'd be late for practice.

Ask the rest of the students what "first feelings" they noticed. Write all the responses on the board, including those that were revealed in the role play. Ask the students to help you think of additional situations involving surprise or spontaneous confrontations and invite volunteers to role play those, too. Coach the volunteers to help them with their active listening responses. Facilitate discussion, reinforcing these guidelines:

- When someone confronts you, respond by active listening. Listen for as long as necessary, allowing the person to blow off steam.
- When listening, don't simply hear the words, listen for the feelings.

Offer feedback to let the person know you hear, and to give the speaker an opportunity to correct your perceptions.
- If the person expresses a lot of anger, see if you can pick up clues as to the person's "first feelings." If you can, feed those back. See if you can help the person acknowledge those feelings.

Next, elaborate on the concept of the <u>planned</u> confrontation. Ask the students under what circumstances they might want to plan a confrontation. Discuss their ideas. If no one mentions it, point out that confronting or re-confronting a conflict situation may be necessary in order to move the conflict toward a resolution using one or more strategies. Say to the students: *Think of it like a play in football. In the huddle the quarterback (that's you) calls the play (decides what strategy to use), but nothing happens until the ball is snapped (the confrontation). In the confrontation itself, use a strong I-message to state your perception of the situation, your feelings, and your desire to find a solution to the problem. Immediately following your confrontation, shift to active listening in order to help the other person express his or her perceptions, feelings, and desires, too.*

Have volunteers role play several examples of planned confrontations. Either have the students think of real conflict situations from their own experience, or refer to "Conflict Scenarios" (page 111). Lead a culminating discussion.

Discussion Questions:

1. What are the benefits of being able to effectively manage a confrontation?
2. Why is it helpful to shift to active listening after you confront someone?
3. How difficult do you think it will be to control your response to a confrontation? . . . What can you do to help yourself get ready?

Criticism — Just Handle It!
Dyads and Discussion

Objectives:

Students will:
— describe a recent criticism they received.
— explain why criticism is often perceived as threatening.
— examine and discuss a four-step process for dealing effectively with criticism.

Materials:

whiteboard

Information to share:

- Some people handle criticism well, but most are threatened by it to some degree.
- The brain reacts to any perceived threat by releasing chemicals into the blood stream. Buying time (the first rule of conflict management) gives these chemicals a chance to dissipate so that negative feelings can begin to go away.
- Use active listening to consciously hear and consider a criticism. If the criticism is valid, say so. You may want to thank the person.
- If you don't understand the criticism, ask questions to get more specific information and greater clarification.

- If you decide that the criticism is *not* true, either 1) reaffirm your position with an I-message and answer any questions the other person may have, or 2) merely acknowledge the person for sharing and disregard the criticism.

Directions:

Prior to class, write the following discussion topic on the board:

"A Recent Criticism I Received"

Begin the activity by announcing that the class is going to be examining a type of communication that people give each other all the time, even though practically no one likes to receive it. Quite often this type of communication leads to conflict. Announce that the subject of the activity is *criticism*.

Have the students choose partners and move their desks or chairs together so they can talk quietly. Then, draw their attention to the topic on the board. Direct the partners to take 1-2 minutes each to speak to this topic. When it is their turn to listen, they should do so attentively, without interrupting. When it is their turn to speak, they should describe the criticism they received, the "first feelings" they experienced upon hearing it, and how they responded. Reassure the students that it doesn't matter whether the criticism was true or untrue. The validity of the criticism should not be the focus of sharing.

When the dyads are finished, generate a class discussion using these questions:

— *How did you respond to the criticism you described?*
— *If the criticism led to a conflict, how could it have been avoided?*

Next, write the following guidelines on the board:

STEPS IN HANDLING CRITICISM

1. BUY YOURSELF SOME TIME!!!!!

2. If the criticism is true, agree.

3. If you are unsure, ask for specifics and clarification.

4. If it is not true, state and reaffirm your position, or simply ignore the criticism.

Go over the steps with the class, inviting student input and examples, and elaborating on each point (see "Information to Share"). Stress the benefits of using active listening and I-messages appropriately. Conclude the activity with a general discussion.

Discussion Questions:

1. What is the most common reaction or "first feeling" associated with receiving criticism and why do we feel it? (defensiveness—because we are threatened)
2. What role does buying time play in turning the receipt of criticism into a positive experience?
3. What can happen if we don't manage criticism well?

Extension:

Have the students practice the four-step process by role playing the situations they shared in their dyads. Conduct at least two demonstration role plays in front of the class, utilizing volunteers. Provide appropriate coaching and reinforcement. Then allow the students to return to their dyads for practice.

Managing Moods
Experience Sheet and Discussion

Objectives:

The students will:
— explain how moods are affected by the residual feelings of conflict.
— identify problems and feelings associated with specific conflicts.
— describe strategies for releasing residual feelings and managing negative moods.

Materials:

one copy of the experience sheet, "Three Lousy Moods," for each student; whiteboard; 3" x 5" index cards

Information to share:

• The feelings we take away from a conflict (*residual* feelings) tend to stay with us for some time. Even a well-managed conflict is stressful, and associated residual feelings carry over into other activities and relationships. In addition, they can be hard on us physically.

• Internal conflicts, or conflicts that cannot be immediately resolved for one reason or another also produce stress. Associated negative feelings may be with us constantly until the problem can be resolved.

• Residual feelings and the feelings associated with ongoing unresolved conflict affect our moods.

• The use of *mood-management* strategies can help us relieve stress and negative feelings, lessening the chance that a "bad mood" will result in damage to our body, our relationships, and other areas of our life.

Directions:

Begin by asking the students: *Have you ever been in an extremely bad mood because of something negative that happened in one relatively small area of your life ?*

Invite volunteers to briefly share their "bad mood" experiences. Then, ask for a show of hands from students who have behaved badly toward a friend or family member for no particular reason other than the fact that they were in a bad mood. Point out that this sort of thing happens all the time.

Distribute the experience sheets and quickly go over the directions. Tell the students to break up into groups of two's or three's and work together to complete their sheets.

Take a few minutes to discuss the three scenarios described on the experience sheet. Looking at one scenario at a time, ask the students how they answered the questions. Help the students recognize and describe how Ahmad, Rita, and Mike each started with a specific problem or conflict which produced certain feelings (frustration, worry, disappointment, anxiety, embarrassment, etc.). In all three cases, these first feelings were followed by anger, and the anger carried over into unrelated activities involving unsuspecting friends.

Write the following guidelines on the board:

GUIDE TO MANAGING MOODS

1. BUY YOURSELF SOME TIME!!!!!

2. Fill this time with <u>mood management strategies</u>.

3. It takes time for feelings to naturally dissipate. Don't let them affect other significant activities or undertakings.

Ask the students: Why is it so important to *"buy time" when you are experiencing negative feelings associated with a problem or conflict?*

Facilitate a discussion around the three guidelines, making additional points, and inviting input and examples from the students (see "Information to Share").

On the board, write the heading, **"Mood Management Strategies."** Ask the students to help you brainstorm positive, healthy ways of releasing anger and other negative feelings. List all ideas. Include items such as:

- Talk with a trusted friend or adult.
- Run laps around the block or track.
- Leave the situation and take several slow, deep breaths.
- Get something to eat or drink.
- Listen to relaxing music.
- Take a walk in a pleasant natural setting.
- Imagine being in a favorite place.
- Work on a project or hobby.

Give each student a 3" x 5" card. Suggest that the students write down three or four mood management ideas that they think might work for them. Encourage them to carry the card with them, or tape it to a mirror or closet door at home as a reminder.

Every week or so, ask volunteers to report on their progress using mood management strategies. Frequently remind the students that these strategies are short-term controls, not permanent solutions to big problems. However, they do relieve stress and allow us to enter into problem solving and conflict resolution with greater self-control and productivity.

Three Lousy Moods
Experience Sheet

Read the following scenarios carefully and answer the questions.

Scenario 1:

Ahmad was just finishing a report on the computer when he hit the wrong key and erased all of his work. He felt totally frustrated and starting to get angry with himself, but he had to get to his next class. Ahmad walked out of the computer room and down the hall. Lost in his thoughts about doing something so stupid, he stumbled right into Judy, knocking her books all over the floor. Then he gave her a disgusted look and yelled, "Why don't you look where you're going?"

Questions:

—What was Ahmad's real problem? _____

_____

—What were his first feelings about that problem? _____

_____

—What were some of his other feelings? _____

_____

—What did Judy do that caused Ahmad to behave toward her the way he did?

_____

—Why did Ahmad yell at Judy? _____

_____

Scenario 2:

Rita was ready to leave for school, but she couldn't find her books and nobody seemed to know where they were. She had two assignments due that day and both were inside her books. She started to get upset. After nearly thirty minutes of searching, Rita found the books in one of her little sister, Martha's, favorite hiding places. When she confronted her, Martha admitted hiding them. Even though she found her books, Rita was still mad at her sister and left for school late and in a terrible mood. When she walked into her first class, her best friend Cathy said, "Hi girl, you look upset." Rita snapped, "Leave me alone, I don't want to talk to you!"

Questions:

—What was Rita's real problem? _____

_____

—What were her first feelings about that problem? _____

_____

—What were some of her other feelings? _____

_____

—What did Cathy do that caused Rita to respond the way she did? _____

_____

—Why did Rita snap at Cathy? _____

_____

Scenario 3:

Mike just found out that he didn't make the final cut for the basketball team. As he walked away from the gym, he started feeling angry. Mike thought it was unfair that some of the guys who did make the team couldn't shoot or maneuver nearly as well as he could. He felt crummy. When he walked around the corner, Mike saw a bunch of his friends talking. When Charlie saw Mike, he said, "What are you looking so down about?" Mike was embarrassed. He didn't want anyone to know he'd been cut, so all he said was, "None of your business," and walked off.

Questions:

—What was Mike's real problem? _____

_____

—What were his first feelings about that problem? _____

_____

—What were some of his other feelings? _____

_____

—What did Charlie do that caused Mike to behave the way he did? _____

_____

—Why was Mike rude to his friends, and why did he just walk off? _____

_____

Bringing It All Together
Practice Exercises

Objectives:

The students will:
— practice the skills of conflict resolution through various forms of behavioral rehearsal.

Materials:

video camera for video production activity; magazines, newspapers, and/or books or computers for reading assignments; writing materials for creative writing activities; art materials of various kinds for cartooning

---

Directions:

The more opportunities you can give students to practice the skills of conflict resolution, the greater the probability that they will internalize those skills. Behavioral rehearsal is the key to producing lasting change. This book contains many role-playing activities. The ideas listed below represent variations in the standard approach to role-play, as well as other practice techniques appropriate for secondary classrooms and counseling groups.

Solution Role Plays

Describe a typical conflict situation to the class. Choose volunteers to play the roles and have them act out the scenario. Interrupt them, however, before the characters resolve their problem. Then form small groups and ask each group to define the conflict, brainstorm possible solutions, and choose the one they feel is the best. Have each group role play its version of the conflict and solution for the rest of the class.

The Freeze Technique

Examine individual behaviors within a dramatized conflict by stopping the action at key points in order to point out how the conflict may escalate or de-escalate because of an attitude, a small action, a failure to listen, and so on. After you stop the action by saying, "freeze," ask the characters why they're behaving the way they are. Ask specific questions such as, "What did (Hector) say or do that you are reacting to?"

Role Reversal.

Changing roles helps students explore both sides of a conflict. This is particularly effective if the conflict is a real one from their own experience. After the students finish role-playing a scenario, have them switch roles and repeat the dramatization. Afterward, ask the students what they learned from experiencing the other person's point of view. Ask them to compare their respective approaches to resolving the problem. Which solution seemed preferable? Why?

Alter Ego

This technique helps students look at possible feelings and motives underlying the actions of various characters in a role play. Station a student, or "alter ego," next to each of the disputants in the conflict scenario. After a character speaks, allow his or her alter ego to add comments that express what the character is actually thinking and/or feeling.

Video Playback

Whenever possible, have a student video your role-playing sessions. View the videos as part of the debriefing and discussion. Stop the video whenever students see something they want to comment on or question. When you come to a particularly pivotal moment in the scenario, replay that segment. In addition, use the video to focus on the importance of body language. Note how the characters stand, the way their posture changes in response to verbal exchanges, etc.

Reading Conflict Stories

Have the students locate conflict stories in magazines, newspapers, or on the internet and identify the main conflicts in novels and short stories. Have them work in two's or three's to analyze the conflict and report to the class concerning its source, the needs of the disputants, the nature of the problem and all its parts, possible or actual resolutions, and alternatives that were not chosen.

Writing Conflict Stories

In small groups, have the students tell about real conflicts they have experienced. Next, have the groups pick one conflict and orally develop it into a fictional story, adding characters, plot twists, and information related to the development and resolution of the conflict. Limit the time and encourage creativity. Have the groups share their stories with the class. Then have the students work individually or in pairs to write stories based on other conflicts that were related in their group. In addition to sharing and discussing the conflicts portrayed, treat these papers as you would any creative writing assignment.

Cartooning Conflict Scenarios

Create a template containing at least four empty cartoon frames. Make copies and distribute them to the students. Have the students work in groups of three or four to fill in the first two frames of their sheet with cartoon characters involved in a conflict. Then have the groups switch cartoons. Tell them to read their new cartoon and create a resolution to the conflict, illustrating that resolution in the final frames.

An alternative is for you to illustrate the first frames of the cartoon before duplicating, setting up the conflict scenario yourself. Then give the same scenario to all groups. Have the groups post and compare their completed cartoon resolutions.

Pictures or illustrations cut from magazines can also evoke conflict scenarios. Choose pictures that contain no words at all, but show strong feelings and suggest a variety of possible "plots." Duplicate these pictures and allow the students to decide what is going on in each one. Suggest that they add cartoon bubbles with dialogue. Have them fill subsequent frames with their own drawings, which show the conflict escalating, de-escalating, and being resolved with specific conflict resolution strategies.

Conflict Scenarios
Additional Fodder for Role Playing

Objectives:

The students will:
— practice the skills of conflict resolution by participating in a variety of role plays and dramatizations.

Materials:

simple props where appropriate; video recording equipment (optional)

Directions:

Use these scenarios as role-play starters. Keep a few copies on hand in case your students have trouble generating conflict scenarios of their own.

———

Stephanie and Robert are playing on the basketball court. Mike asks if he can play. Robert says, "Sure!" at the same time that Stephanie whispers, "No!" Stephanie doesn't like Mike but doesn't want to be rude, so instead she starts hogging the ball and sulking.

———

Jan is reading a magazine at home in the evening. Her brother Dave wants to read the same magazine, so he tricks her into laying it down on the coffee table and then takes it. They start to fight loudly.

———

Alex and Wally are working on a report together, but every time they get together, Alex comes prepared and Wally doesn't. Wally forgets to read the material, or loses his notes, or has some other excuse. Alex, who ends up doing most of the work, complains to his dad, who tells him he'll have to confront the problem. That means confronting Wally.

———

When Donna misses a play in softball, Joy makes a face and says something under her breath. Later, in gym, she loudly refers to Donna as a fat cow. The next day in the hallway, Donna knocks the books out of Joy's arms, then steps on the books and laughs. The two start to fight. When a teacher approaches, they quickly agree to meet and "settle things" in the park after school.

_____

Lauren has been spreading rumors that Maria is a shoplifter. She has even described items she's seen at Maria's house that she swears Maria couldn't afford to buy. Other kids are starting to believe the rumors, and now the whole story has gotten back to Maria. She approaches Lauren before class and starts shouting loud accusations and threats.

_____

Tony and Neil share a locker at school. They have been bickering for days. Neil says that Tony is a slob, and is taking up more than his share of the locker space. Tony complains that Neil junks up the locker with stuff from his science experiments and that some of the compounds smell.

_____

Brian has saved almost enough money to buy his first car. For the past year, ever since he got his license, his older sister, Jodi, has let Brian borrow her car when he really needs one. One night Brian uses Jodi's car and forgets to lock it. The next morning it's gone. Jodi insists that the insurance company won't pay her enough to replace her car. She wants the money in Brian's car fund, too. Brian refuses. Their parents insist that Brian and Jodi will have to work it out.

_____

Diane and Jean have been best friends all through school. But now Diane feels like Jean is becoming closer to Chris, her new neighbor. This past weekend, she didn't hear from Jean at all. On Monday morning, she finds out that Jean and Chris went to the mall together on Saturday and the movies on Sunday. When Jean says, "Hi," to her during third period, Diane ignores her and walks away. When Jean teasingly calls Diane stuck up, Diane turns and yells at her to drop dead. They start to argue.

_____

Lupe and Jessie are co-chairs of the prom committee, but they haven't been getting along. Lupe has made several decisions without consulting Jessie, which makes Jessie feel left out and resentful. Lupe complains that Jessie has been too busy with sports and hasn't been around to help her. She thinks she's been carrying most of the load. At this point, the two are avoiding each other, which is starting to jeopardize the prom itself.

———

Kim has been ignoring Lonnie's barbs and ridicules for months, but inside she is seething. She feels that Lonnie is trying to turn the other kids against her by drawing attention to her clothes, the way she walks, her thin legs, her old bicycle—everything. Now other kids in Lonnie's group are starting to snicker when she's around. Kim has just about reached her limit.

———

Hoa's parents are disgusted by what they call her "punk look." One day when she comes home from school, Hoa finds half the clothes gone from her closet and dresser drawers. When she confronts her mother, Hoa is told that as long as she lives in her parents home, she will have to dress according to their wishes.

———

Roy promises to take his two younger brothers to the game on Friday night. This pleases Roy's parents, because they've been hoping to have an evening to themselves. However, on Friday afternoon, several of Roy's friends decide to have a pre-game barbecue and then all sit together during the game. When Roy gets home, he tells his younger brothers that he has to work the concession stand at the game and can't take them. His father overhears, calls the school, finds out Roy is lying, and threatens to ground him for a month.

———

When Olivia's parents agreed to let her buy Oscar, her big German Shepherd, they made her promise to give him regular baths, keep his bed clean, and vacuum the carpets twice a week to prevent fleas. But Olivia has been busy and has neglected her chores. Now Oscar is covered with fleas and has a skin condition that the vet says will be expensive to cure. Today, Olivia's parents matter-of-factly announce that they are going to give Oscar away.

———

Lisa wants to invite Miguel to her club's big party, but she's concerned he may refuse, so she talks it over with her friend, Rosie. Rosie then tells Linda, knowing that Linda wants to invite Miguel, too. When Lisa finds out that Linda has already asked Miguel, she figures out what happened, and accuses Rosie of betraying a trust. Rosie coldly responds that Lisa's plans were never a secret.

Sharing Circles

The Sharing Circle is one of the most powerful and versatile of the instructional strategies used in this curriculum. The purpose of the Sharing Circle is to promote growth and development in the areas of communication, self-awareness, personal mastery, and interpersonal skills.

Using Sharing Circles with students and educators world wide has demonstrated the power of the Sharing Circle in contributing to the development of conflict resolution skills. Circles can noticeably accelerate the development and internalization of the conflict strategies introduced in this book.

They are a key ingredient in bringing about the growth necessary for students to engage in the level of *self*-management required to effectively manage and resolve conflict.

This section contains twenty fully developed Sharing Circles, along with all of the information you need to become a skilled circle facilitator. Please do not attempt to lead a circle until you have read this introductory material. Then use circles liberally, allowing their innumerable benefits to venerate every aspect of your conflict program.

An Overview of the Sharing Circle

The Sharing Circle is a unique small-group discussion process in which participants (including the leader) share their feelings, experiences, and insights in response to specific, assigned topics. They are loosely structured, and participants are expected to adhere to rules that promote the goals of the circle while assuring cooperation, effective communication, trust, and confidentiality.

To take full advantage of this process there are some things to be aware of.

First, the topic elaborations provided under the heading, "Introduce the Topic," are guides for you to follow when presenting the topic to your students. They are excellent models, but they need not be read verbatim. The idea is to focus the attention of students on the specific topic to be discussed. In your elaboration, try to use language and examples that are appropriate to the age, ability, and culture of your students.

Second, we strongly urge you to respect the integrity of the sharing and discussion phases of the circle. These two phases are procedurally and qualitatively different, yet of equal importance in promoting awareness, insight, and higher-level thinking in students. After you have led several circles, you will appreciate the instructional advantage of maintaining this unique relationship.

All Sharing Circle topics are intended to develop awareness and insight through voluntary sharing. The discussion questions allow students to understand what has been shared at deeper levels, to evaluate ideas that have been generated by the topic, and to apply specific concepts to other areas of learning.

As students follow the rules and relate to each other verbally during the Sharing Circle, they are practicing oral communication and learning to listen. Through insights developed in the course of pondering and discussing the various topics, students are offered the opportunity to grow in awareness and to feel more masterful—more in control of their feelings, thoughts, and behaviors. Through the positive experience of give and take, they learn more about effective modes of social interaction. This is a firm foundation upon which to build conflict resolution skills and strategies.

The Sharing Circle topics offered here address human relations competencies, such as the ability to include others, assume and share responsibility, offer help, behave assertively, solve problems, resolve conflicts, etc. Such topics elevate awareness in the human relations domain and encourage students to more effectively exercise these competencies and skills each day. The first step in a student's developing any competency is knowing that he or she is capable of demonstrating it. The Sharing Circle is particularly adept at helping students to recognize and acknowledge their own capabilities.

The Sharing Circle is also a wonderful tool for teaching cooperation. As equitably as possible, the circle structure attempts to meet the needs of all participants. Everyone's feelings are accepted. Comparisons and judgements are not made. The circle is not another competitive arena, but is guided by a spirit of collaboration. When students practice fair, respectful interaction with one another, they benefit from the experience and are likely to employ these responsible behaviors in other life situations.

Relating effectively to others is a challenge we all face. People who are effective in their social interactions have the ability to understand others. They know how to interact flexibly, skillfully, and responsibly. At the same time, they recognize their own needs and maintain their own integrity. Socially effective people can process the nonverbal as well as verbal messages of others. They possess the very important awareness that all people have the power to affect one another. They are aware of not only how others affect them, but the effects their behaviors have on others. All of these skills and awarenesses are vital in conflict resolution.

The Sharing Circle process has been designed so that healthy, responsible behaviors are modeled by the teacher or counselor in his or her role as circle leader. The rules also require that the students relate positively and effectively to one another. The Sharing Circle brings out and affirms the positive qualities inherent in everyone and allows students to practice effective modes of communication. Because Sharing Circles provide a place where participants are listened to and their feelings accepted, students learn how to provide the same conditions to peers and adults outside the circle.

Through this sharing of interpersonal experiences, students learn that behavior can be positive or negative, and sometimes both at the same time. Consequences can be constructive, destructive, or both. Different people respond differently to the same event. They have different feelings and thoughts. The students begin to understand what will cause what to happen; they grasp the concept of cause and effect; they see themselves affecting others and being affected by others.

The ability to make accurate interpretations and responses in social interactions allows students to know where they stand with themselves and with others. They can tell what actions "fit" a situation. Sharing Circles are marvelous testing grounds where students can observe themselves and others in action, and can begin to see themselves as contributing to the good and bad feelings of others. With this understanding, students are helped to conclude that being responsible towards others feels good, and is the most valuable and personally rewarding form of interaction.

Circles can noticeably accelerate the development and internalization of the conflict resolution skills and strategies introduced in this book. They are a key ingredient in bringing about the growth necessary for students to engage in the level of *self*-management required to effectively manage and resolve conflict.

How to Set Up Sharing Circles

Group Size and Composition

Sharing Circles are a time for focusing on individual contributions in an unhurried fashion. For this reason, each Sharing Circle group needs to be kept relatively small—eight to twelve usually works best. Young people of middle and high-school age are capable of extensive verbalization, and you will want to encourage this, not stifle them because of time constraints.

Each group should be as heterogeneous as possible with respect to sex, ability, and racial/ethnic background. Sometimes there will be a group in which all the students are particularly reticent to speak. At these times, bring in an expressive student or two who will get things going. Sometimes it is necessary for practical reasons to change the membership of a group. Once established, however, it is advisable to keep a group as stable as possible.

Length and Location of Sharing Circles

Circles can last from 15 to 30 minutes depending on the number of students participating in the circle and how comfortable they have become at sharing. At first students tend to be reluctant to express themselves fully because they do not yet know that the circle is a safe place. Consequently your first sessions may not last more than 10 minutes. Generally speaking, students become comfortable and motivated to speak with continued experience.

In a classroom setting, Sharing Circles may be conducted at any time during the class period. Starting Sharing Circles at the beginning of the period allows additional time in case students become deeply involved in the topic. If you start circles late in the period, make sure the students are aware of their responsibility to be concise.

In all settings, Sharing Circles may be carried out wherever there is room for students to sit in a circle and experience few or no distractions. Some leaders conduct sessions outdoors, with students seated in a secluded, grassy area. When conducted indoors, chairs provide the most popular seating solution, however, students may like to sit on the floor, especially if there is carpet and they can sit comfortably.

How to Lead a Sharing Circle

This section is a thorough guide for conducting Sharing Circles. It covers major points to keep in mind and answers questions which will arise as you begin using the program. Please remember that these guidelines are presented to assist you, not to restrict you. Follow them, and trust your own leadership style at the same time.

The Sharing Circle is a structured communication process that provides students a safe place for learning about life and developing important aspects of social-emotional learning.

First, we'll provide a brief overview of the process of leading a Sharing Circle and then we'll cover each step in more detail.

A Sharing Circle begins when a group of students and the adult leader sit down together in a circle so that each person is able to see the others easily. The leader of the Sharing Circle briefly greets and welcomes each individual, conveying a feeling of enthusiasm blended with seriousness.

When everyone appears comfortable, the leader takes a few moments to review the Sharing Circle Rules. These rules inform the students of the positive behaviors required of them and guarantees the emotional safety and security, and equality of each member.

After the students understand and agree to follow the rules, the leader announces the topic for the session. A brief elaboration of the topic follows in which the leader provides examples and possibly mentions the topics relationship to prior topics or to other things the students are involved in. Then the leader re-states the topic and allows a little silence during which circle members may review and ponder their own related memories and mentally prepare their verbal response to the topic. (The topics and elaborations are provided.)

Next, the leader invites the circle participants to voluntarily share their responses to the topic, one at a time. No one is forced to share, but everyone is given an opportunity to share while all the other circle members listen attentively. The circle participants tell the group about themselves, their personal experiences, thoughts, feelings, hopes and dreams as they relate to the topic. Most of the circle time is devoted to this sharing phase because of its central importance.

During this time, the leader assumes a dual role—that of leader and participant. The leader makes sure that everyone who wishes to speak is given the opportunity while simultaneously enforcing the rules as necessary. The leader also takes a turn to speak if he or she wishes.

After everyone who wants to share has done so, the leader introduces the next phase of the Sharing Circle by asking several discussion questions. This phase represents a transition to the intellectual mode and allows participants to reflect on and express learnings gained from the sharing phase and encourages participants to combine cognitive abilities and emotional experiencing. It's in this phase that participants are able to crystallize learnings and to understand the relevance of the discussion to their daily lives. (Discussion questions for each topic are provided.)

When the students have finished discussing their responses to the questions and the session has reached a natural closure, the leader ends the session. The leader thanks the students for being part of the Sharing Circle and states that it is over.

What follows is a more detailed look at the process of leading a Sharing Circle.

Steps for Leading a Sharing Circle

1. Welcome Sharing Circle members

2. Review the Sharing Circle rules (optional after the first few sessions)

3. Introduce the topic

4. Sharing by circle members

5. Ask discussion questions

6. Close the circle

1. Welcome Sharing Circle members

As you sit down with the students in a Sharing Circle group, remember that you are not teaching a lesson. You are facilitating a group of people. Establish a positive atmosphere. In a relaxed manner, address each student by name, using eye contact and conveying warmth. An attitude of seriousness blended with enthusiasm will let the students know that this Sharing Circle group is an important learning experience—an activity that can be interesting and meaningful.

2. Review the Sharing Circle rules

At the beginning of the first Sharing Circle, and at appropriate intervals thereafter, go over the rules for the circle. They are:

Sharing Circle Rules

* Everyone gets a turn to share, including the leader.

* You can skip your turn if you wish.

* Listen to the person who is sharing.

* There are no interruptions, probing, put-downs, or gossip.

* Share the time equally.

From this point on, demonstrate to the students that you expect them to remember and abide by the ground rules. Convey that you think well of them and know they are fully capable of responsible behavior. Let them know that by coming to the Sharing Circle they are making a commitment to listen and show acceptance and respect for the other students and you. It is helpful to write the rules on chart paper and keep them on display for the benefit of each Sharing Circle session.

3. Introduce the topic

State the topic, and then in your own words, elaborate and provide examples as each lesson in this book suggests. The introduction or elaboration of the topic is designed to get students focused and thinking about how they will respond to the topic. By providing more than just the mere statement of the topic, the elaboration gives students a few moments to expand their thinking and to make a personal connection to the topic at hand. Add clarifying statements of your own that will help the students understand the topic. Answer questions about the topic, and emphasize that there are no "right" responses. Finally, restate the topic, opening the session to responses (theirs and yours). Sometimes taking your turn first helps the students understand the aim of the topic. The introductions, as written in this book, are provided to give you some general ideas for opening the Sharing Circle. It's important that you adjust and modify the introduction and elaboration to suit the ages, abilities, levels, cultural/ethnic backgrounds and interests of your students.

4. Sharing by circle members

The most important point to remember is this: The purpose of these Sharing Circles is to give students an opportunity to express themselves and be accepted for the experiences, thoughts, and feelings they share. Avoid taking the action away from the students. They are the stars!

5. Ask discussion questions

Responding to discussion questions is the cognitive portion of the process. During this phase, the leader asks thought-provoking questions to stimulate free discussion and higher-level thinking. Each Sharing Circle lesson in this book concludes with several discussion questions. At times, you may want to formulate questions that are more appropriate to the level of understanding in your students—or to what was actually shared in the circle. If you wish to make connections between the topic and your content area, ask questions that will accomplish that objective and allow the answering of the discussion questions to extend longer.

6. Close the circle

The ideal time to end a Sharing Circle is when the discussion question phase reaches natural closure. Sincerely thank everyone for being part of the circle. Don't thank specific students for speaking, as doing so might convey the impression that speaking is more appreciated than mere listening. Then close the group by saying, "This Sharing Circle is over," or "OK, that ends our circle."

NOTE:

More information on Sharing Circles and additional topics are available in *THE SHARING CIRCLE HANDBOOK* (Innerchoice Publishing, 2010) or online at www.InnerchoicePublishing.com

Steps for Leading a Sharing Circle

1. **Welcome Sharing Circle members**

2. **Review the Sharing Circle rules**
   (Optional after the first few sessions)

3. **Introduce the topic:**

4. **Sharing by circle members**

5. **Ask discussion questions**

6. **Close the circle**

Sharing Circle Rules

✳ **Everyone gets a turn to share, including the leader.**

✳ **You can skip your turn if you wish.**

✳ **Listen to the person who is speaking.**

✳ **There are no interruptions, probing, put-downs, or gossip.**

✳ **Share the time equally.**

A Time I Listened Well to Someone

A Sharing Circle

Objectives:

The students will:
— describe a time when they listened effectively.
— identify effective listening behaviors.

Introduce the Topic:

Most of us appreciate having someone really listen to us. In this session we are going to turn this idea around and talk about how it feels to listen to someone else. The topic is, "A Time I Listened Well to Someone."

Can you remember a time when you really paid attention to someone and listened carefully to what he or she said. This means that you didn't interrupt with your own ideas or daydream about your own plans, but really concentrated and tried to understand what the other person was attempting to get across. Maybe you've listened to a friend like that, or a younger brother or sister, or a teacher or coach. Think about it for a few moments and, if you wish, tell us about, "A Time I Listened Well to Someone."

Discussion Questions:

1. What kinds of things make listening difficult?
2. Why is it important to listen to others?
3. What could you do to improve your listening?
4. How do you feel when someone really listens to you?

A Time When Someone Wouldn't Listen to Me
A Sharing Circle

Objectives:

The students will:
— describe incidents involving poor communication.
— distinguish between lack of listening skill and lack of interest.
— explain how conflicts develop from failures to listen.

Introduce the Topic:

Have you ever needed very much to have someone listen to you, and been unable to get that person's attention? It can be very frustrating, even maddening, to try to communicate with a person who refuses to listen. Today, we're going to share examples of this type of problem. Our topic is, "A Time When Someone Wouldn't Listen to Me."

Think of an occasion when you really wanted to talk with a specific person. Perhaps you needed to discuss a problem, or were eager to tell this person an exciting story, or maybe you had a rather complicated question that you needed to ask. Regardless of your reason for wanting to talk, this person refused to listen. Tell us how you felt and what affect the incident had on your relationship with the person. Please don't mention any names. Our topic is, "A Time When Someone Wouldn't Listen to Me."

Discussion Questions:

1. How did most of us feel when we weren't listened to?
2. Did these people bluntly refuse to listen, or were they just poor listeners? What's the difference?
3. Did any of these situations lead to conflict? How do such conflicts develop?
4. What insights have you gained into your own listening habits from this topic?

A Person I Feel Safe With
A Sharing Circle

Objectives:

The students will:
— identify safe and accepting relationships.
— describe specific behaviors that contribute to secure relationships.

Introduce the Topic:

Today our topic is, "A Person I Feel Safe With." The world can seem like a pretty hostile place at times, with crowding, crime, and conflict between people and groups. Even in our daily lives, we experience the stress of competition and the press of time as we try to juggle our relationships and responsibilities. All of this makes it especially important that we have people in our lives with whom we can relax, knowing that we are safe and secure—not just physically, but emotionally. Who is such a person in your life? Tell us about someone who gives you a good feeling, who accepts and supports you, and always causes you to feel safe. This person could be an adult, child, parent, relative, or friend. Tell us specifically what the person does to cause you to feel secure in his or her presence. The topic is, "A Person I Feel Safe With."

Discussion Questions:

1. What were the main reasons we gave for feeling safe with the people we described?
2. How do you know when someone accepts you just the way you are?
3. How can we become people with whom others feel safe?
4. Does feeling safe with a person mean that you and that person never disagree or experience conflicts? Explain.

Something I Knew I Could Do
A Sharing Circle

Objectives:

The students will:
— identify an area in which they have self-confidence.
— describe how self-trust and self-confidence develop.

Introduce the Topic:

Our topic for this session is, "Something I Knew I Could Do." Have you ever faced a task you knew you could accomplish, or a challenge you knew in advance you could master? ...and then went on to prove it? Tell us about such a time. Perhaps you learned a new game or computer program, or athletic skill. Maybe you completed a tough assignment or got an A on a test. Or maybe you built something that required a lot of time and effort. What were your feelings, and where did your confidence come from? Take a minute to think about it and then tell us about a time you trusted completely your ability to get something done. The topic is, "Something I Knew I Could Do."

Discussion Questions:

1. How did you feel having that kind of trust in yourself?
2. How did you develop so much confidence in that area?
3. How can you learn to trust yourself as much in other areas?

I Played a Game and the Other Side Won

A Sharing Circle

Objectives:

The students will:
— discuss the dynamics of winning and losing and their relationship to conflict.
— identify strategies for handling internal and external conflicts that arise in win-lose situations.

Introduce the topic:

We win some games, and we lose some. Both in sports and in other types of games, the law of averages doesn't always work in our favor. Today we're going to talk about some of the losing times. Our topic is, "I Played a Game and the Other Side Won."

Think of a time when you were on the losing side. Maybe the game involved just one other person, like a tennis match or a game of Monopoly. Or maybe you were a member of a football, basketball, soccer, or track team. How did you feel when your opponent won? What did you do? Were you very upset or did you take it in stride and tell yourself that you'd win the next game? Think about it for a few moments. The topic is, "I Played a Game and the Other Side Won."

Discussion Questions:

1. How did most of us feel when we lost?
2. Did a conflict occur when you lost the game, or do you think the game itself was a conflict? Explain.
3. What can we learn from our reactions to losing games that will help us better handle more serious conflicts?
4. How can we maintain a win-win attitude, even in win-lose situations?

A Time Someone Betrayed My Trust

A Sharing Circle

Objectives:

The students will:
— identify factors that contribute to trust in a relationship.
— explain how a betrayal of trust can lead to conflict.
— describe how trust is developed.

Introduce the Topic:

Our topic for this session concerns something that can very quickly lead to conflict. The topic is, "A Time Someone Betrayed My Trust."

Have you ever trusted another person with something, or maybe shared a secret, and that person somehow betrayed your trust? Perhaps you loaned a friend something you valued — a book, computer game, article of clothing, your car — and your friend didn't take care of it properly. Or maybe you told something to a person in strict confidence and then found out later that he or she repeated your secret to several other people. Another possibility is that someone promised to do something for you — pick you up, run an errand, turn in your library book, loan you some money — and then failed to follow through. Without mentioning names, tell us what happened and how you felt. Our topic is, "A Time Someone Betrayed My Trust."

Discussion Questions:

1. Did the incident you shared cause a conflict between you and the other person?
2. Why is trust such an important part of any close relationship?
3. How is trust developed?
4. If you really want someone to trust you and you betray that trust just once, what does it take for the person to trust you again?

Something That Really Bothers Me

A Sharing Circle

Objectives:

The students will:
— identify an internal conflict they are experiencing.
— describe feelings associated with internal conflict.
— describe strategies for dealing with internal conflict.

Introduce the Topic:

Everybody is bothered at one time or another about something. We can be bothered by the need to make a tough decision, or by a decision we already made that seems to have turned out poorly. Sometimes we're bothered by events that are going on in our neighborhood, our nation, or the world. And sometimes we're bothered by a simple doubt, like whether or not we put the dog out before we left for school.

Have you ever been bothered by the behavior of a friend or relative? Have you ever felt a nagging fear that you did something to upset someone, but couldn't put your finger on what it was? There are lots of things that can bother us deep inside. These are examples of internal conflict, and it often helps to talk about them. Take a moment to think. When you are ready, our topic is, "Something That Really Bothers Me."

Discussion Questions:

1. What kinds of things seemed to bother must of us?
2. What can we do to relieve the feelings that accompany internal conflicts like these?
3. If you could do anything you wanted about the situation you described, what would you do?

I Observed a Conflict
A Sharing Circle

Objectives:

The students will:
— describe a conflict situation they observed.
— discuss the dynamics of conflict.
— describe feelings generated in conflict situations.

Introduce the Topic:

Today we're going to talk about conflict situations we've witnessed. Our topic is, "I Observed a Conflict."

There probably isn't anyone here who hasn't at some point in his or her life watched some kind of conflict taking place. A conflict can take many forms. It can be an argument between two people over who has the best idea for a project, or who needs the car more. It can be a squabble over who gets the last cookie. Some conflicts are fights or arguments that involve some kind of violence or the threat of it. Still other conflicts take place inside one person; for example, when someone is torn between two choices, like who to vote for, what to do on the weekend, or who to live with after a divorce. Think of a conflict that you observed. It could have been between friends, family members, or strangers. Without actually telling us who was involved, or your relationship to the people, tell us what happened. The topic is, "I Observed a Conflict."

Discussion Questions:

1. Why do we have conflicts?
2. What kinds of things happened in most of the conflicts we shared?
3. Why is it sometimes difficult to think clearly when you get involved in an argument?
4. Is it possible for both people to win in a conflict? How?

I Got Into a Conflict
A Sharing Circle

Objectives:

The students will:
— describe conflicts they have experienced and what caused them.
— describe ways of dealing with the feelings of others in conflict situations.
— identify strategies for resolving conflicts with peers and adults.

Introduce the Topic:

Our topic today is, "I Got Into a Conflict." Conflicts are very common. They occur because of big and little things that happen in our lives. And sometimes the littlest things that happen can lead to the biggest conflicts. This is your opportunity to talk about a time when you had an argument or fight with someone. Maybe you and a friend argued over something that one of you said that the other didn't like. Or maybe you argued with a brother or sister over what TV show to watch, or who should do a particular chore around the house. Have you ever had a fight because someone broke a promise or couldn't keep as secret? If you feel comfortable telling us what happened, we'd like to hear it. Describe what the other person did and said, and what you did and said. Tell us how you felt and how the other person seemed to feel. There's just one thing you shouldn't tell us and that's the name of the other person, okay? Take a few moments to think about it. The topic is, "I Got Into a Conflict."

Discussion Questions:

1. How did most of us feel when we were part of a conflict?
2. What kinds of things led to the conflicts that we shared?
3. How could some of our conflicts have been prevented?
4. What conflict management strategies could have been used in the situations that we shared?

I Accidentally Made Somebody Mad

A Sharing Circle

Objectives:

The students will:
— describe incidents involving unexpected eruptions of anger.
— identify ways of controlling their own reactions to anger.

Introduce the Topic:

We all occasionally say or do something that makes someone angry. Quite often we do it unintentionally. We're going to talk about incidents like that today. Our topic is, "I Accidentally Made Somebody Mad."

Think of a time when, without intending to, you caused someone to get very upset. Maybe you slipped and said something you shouldn't have said. Or maybe you were trying to be funny but the other person took your statement as a put-down. Perhaps you brought up a sensitive subject that "pushed a button" for the other person. How did you feel when this happened? Were you able to prevent the incident from turning into a conflict, or did you get angry in return? Tell us what happened without mentioning any names. The topic is, "I Accidentally Made Somebody Mad."

Discussion Questions:

1. What successful strategies did we use to calm the person down in these situations?
2. How can we control our own reactions when suddenly confronted with another person's anger?
3. What did you learn about conflict from this session? ...about conflict prevention? ...about conflict management?

I Was Involved in a Misunderstanding
A Sharing Circle

Objectives:

The students will:
— identify missing information and faulty communication as two main causes of misunderstandings.
— describe ways of handling misunderstandings that can prevent their escalation.

Introduce the topic:

Sometimes conflicts occur because one or both people don't have enough information about each other's ideas, feelings, or actions. They simply don't understand each other. Let's talk about times like these today. Our topic is, "I Was Involved in a Misunderstanding."

Tell us about a time when some piece of information was missing and it caused either you or another person to draw the wrong conclusion. Maybe you didn't understand a friend's reason for making a particular decision, or maybe the friend didn't understand yours. Perhaps you said something that the other person took the wrong way because it was out of context. Or it could have been a situation in which you or the other person misunderstood instructions and ended up doing the wrong thing. Misunderstandings don't have to lead to conflict, but they sometimes do. Tell us how you handled yours. The topic is, "I Was Involved in a Misunderstanding."

Discussion Questions:

1. What strategies for handling misunderstandings seemed to work particularly well in the situations we shared?
2. Since misunderstandings are usually unintentional, what are some things we can do to make sure they don't escalate into conflict?
3. How does good communication figure in the prevention of misunderstandings? ...in their resolution?

Something I Thought Was Funny Made Someone Else Mad

A Sharing Circle

Objectives:

The students will:
— identify types of humor that are potentially offensive.
— explain how offensive humor leads to conflict.
— discuss strategies for responding to conflict produced by offensive humor.

Introduce the topic:

Humorous comments and stories can be a lot of fun, but if they offend anyone, they can also cause a lot of trouble. Today, we're going to talk about some of the negative results of humor. Our topic is, "Something I Thought Was Funny Made Someone Else Mad."

Have you ever repeated a joke that someone thought was offensive? Maybe the joke poked fun at a certain group of people, or at a religious or political belief system. Or maybe you told a story about someone that you thought was clever, but the subject of the story considered it a put-down. Sometimes friends get in the habit of tossing out little barbs and teasing insults. After a while, it gets to be a habit. Think of a time when your attempt at humor backfired. Tell us what happened, but if the joke is offensive, please don't repeat it again here. The topic is, "Something I Thought Was Funny Made Someone Else Mad."

Discussion Questions:

1. From the things we shared, what types of humor would you say tend to get us into trouble?
2. When you realize you've offended someone, how can you prevent a conflict from occurring?
3. Why do people put each other down and consider it funny?
4. If you hear people putting each other down or repeating offensive jokes, what might you do to make them more aware?

A Time Someone Put Me Down, But I Handled It Well

A Sharing Circle

Objectives:

The students will:
— describe positive ways of responding to put-downs.
— explain how put-downs can lead to conflict and violence.

Introduce the Topic:

Our topic today involves some of the language of conflict. It has to do with words — and the way they're spoken — that tend to cause hurt, resentment, and anger. But it also has to do with our ability to control ourselves and prevent conflict. The topic is, "A Time Someone Put Me Down, But I Handled It Well."

Think of a situation in which you felt someone really put you down. Maybe the person called you a name, or made a negative comment about your appearance or something you did. Perhaps you were trying to be friendly with someone and that person rudely rejected you. Maybe the put-down was done unknowingly or as a joke, or perhaps the person did it deliberately. In any case, you were able to withstand the remark and control your emotions and behavior. Tell us how you did that. What did you say to yourself in order to stay "up" when someone put you down. Please don't mention any names. The topic is, "A Time Someone Put Me Down, But I Handled It Well."

Discussion Questions:

1. Why do people put each other down?
2. What effective ways of reacting to put downs did you hear in the circle today?
3. How can a simple put-down lead to violence?
4. What did you learn from this session about preventing conflict? ...about your own communication behaviors?

A Time Someone Took Something Away From Me
A Sharing Circle

Objectives:

The students will:
— describe incidents in which a possession, privilege, or idea was taken from them.
— explain how struggles over ownership lead to conflict.
— identify strategies for dealing with contests over possessions.

Introduce the topic:

Sometimes conflicts occur over possessions — over who owns or has the right to use something. Today we're going to look at what it's like to be on the losing end of an incident like that. Our topic is, "A Time Someone Took Something Away From Me."

Think of a time this happened to you. Maybe a person actually grabbed something out of your hand or your backpack and took off with it. Or maybe a friend took your idea, developed it, and got all the credit. Perhaps someone took the book you were reading and never returned it, or grabbed your place at the lunch table when you went to get a soda. Have you ever had your privileges taken away by your parents? Have you ever had to give up a pet, or a planned activity, or your car keys? Without mentioning names, tell us what happened, how you felt, and how you responded. The topic is, "A Time Someone Took Something Away From Me."

Discussion Questions:

1. What is the first thing you want to do when someone takes something from you?
2. How can you stand up for yourself without causing a conflict?
3. What strategies can you use to resolve a conflict involving ownership or use of something?
4. What have you learned about conflict from this session?

Someone Was Really Mad and Having Trouble, So I Helped

A Sharing Circle

Objectives:

The students will:
— describe incidents in which they intervened in a conflict or its aftermath.
— identify situations in which intervention and mediation may be required to resolve a conflict.

Introduce the Topic:

Our topic today involves our reactions to seeing another person in conflict. The topic is, "Someone Was Really Mad and Having Trouble, So I Helped."

Think of a time when you encountered a friend or family member who was extremely angry about something, which probably had nothing to do with you, yet you felt a desire to help the person. Maybe the person was mad because she or he was trying to get something done and kept running into difficulties. Perhaps the person had just finished arguing with someone. Or maybe the person had recently experienced some kind of failure or disappointment. Whatever the problem was, you stepped in and tried to help. Tell us how you reacted, what you did, and how your efforts were received. Please don't mention any names. The topic is, "Someone Was Really Mad and Having Trouble, So I Helped."

Discussion Questions:

1. What feelings did most of us have that compelled us to get involved?
2. How can you tell if someone is willing to accept your help?
3. How can you help and still be careful not to intervene in potentially dangerous situations?
4. When should you always seek the help of an adult?

When One Person Kept Blaming Another for Causing a Problem

A Sharing Circle

Objectives:

The students will:
— describe a time when blaming perpetuated a conflict.
— state why blaming is counterproductive to conflict resolution.

Introduce the Topic:

Today in our Sharing Circle, we're going to talk about times when we were part of the "blame game." Our topic is, "When One Person Kept Blaming Another for Causing a Problem."

Blaming is something we are all tempted to do at times. But it usually isn't very helpful. Saying a problem is someone else's fault may get us out of trouble, but it usually doesn't solve the problem. Can you think of a time when you saw one person blame another for just about every part of a problem? Maybe you know someone who gets in trouble a lot and always says it's someone else's fault. Or maybe you have a brother or sister who blames you for just about every problem that comes up at home. Have you heard government leaders who always seem to be blaming each other instead of taking responsibility? Have you tried to settle fights between younger

children in which it was hard to figure out what happened because each child blamed the other? Think about it for a few moments. Tell us what happened and how you felt, but don't use any names. The topic is, "When One Person Kept Blaming Another for Causing a Problem."

Discussion Questions:

1. Why is blaming not a helpful thing to do?
2. How do you feel when someone blames you for something?
3. If you're trying to help two people settle a conflict, how can you get them to stop blaming each other?

A Time We Needed Help to Resolve a Conflict

A Sharing Circle

Objectives:

The students will:
— describe a conflict in which the help of a third party was needed.
— identify helpful behaviors on the part of a conflict mediator.

Introduce the Topic:

Our topic for this session is, "A Time We Needed Help to Resolve a Conflict." All of us get into conflicts with our family and friends. Much of the time, we work things out without getting anyone else involved. But sometimes a conflict is too big or too upsetting to handle without help. Can you remember such a time? Maybe you and a brother or sister were arguing over whose turn it was to mow the lawn, and you had to ask one of your parents to help figure it out. Or maybe you had a conflict with a friend over something you were told he or she said about you behind your back, and it took the help of another friend to get the two of you back together. Perhaps you and a classmate had to ask the teacher to settle an argument over who had the correct answer to a problem, or maybe you had to let your coach help settle a fight between you and a teammate. Think about it for a few moments, and tell us what the conflict was about and what the third person did to help you settle it. The topic is, "A Time We Needed Help to Resolve a Conflict."

Discussion Questions:

1. What were some of the reasons that we had to ask for help?
2. When is it a good idea to let someone else help you resolve a conflict?
3. If you ask for help resolving a conflict and the person you ask just comes over and tells you what to do, is that helpful? Why or why not?
4. What kind of help is helpful in resolving a conflict?

A Time I Stood Up for Something I Strongly Believe In

A Sharing Circle

Objectives:

The students will:
— describe times when they behaved assertively regarding a strongly held value or principle.
— demonstrate an understanding of assertive versus nonassertive behaviors.

Introduce the Topic:

Many times during our lives, we are given the opportunity to speak out for the things we believe in. By now, most of us have experienced at least one such occasion. Taking a stand can be a difficult experience, especially if friends or relatives don't agree with our position. Even when they do agree, it's not necessarily easy to state our beliefs publicly. Today, we're going to talk about the conviction and determination these situations demand. Our topic is, "I Stood Up for Something I Strongly Believe In."

Perhaps you saw a group of people doing something that you felt was wrong, and decided that they needed to be confronted. Maybe you observed some kids teasing or harassing another kid, and intervened. Or maybe, during a conversation about a controversial subject, you stated your beliefs even though everyone else in the group held the opposing view. Perhaps you decided to leave a group that had started using drugs, but before you left made sure that everyone knew you thought what they were doing
was wrong and dangerous. One thing is generally true. When we stand up for what we believe in, we feel a sense of pride and accomplishment, and the more often we do it, the greater our courage the next time it happens. If you decide to share, please don't mention the names of the other people involved. The topic is, "I Stood Up for Something I Strongly Believe In."

Discussion Questions:

1. As you look back on the situation you shared, how do you feel about it right now?
2. Why is it sometimes hard to stand up for your beliefs?
3. What are the risks of taking a stand? What are the benefits?
4. What are some ills in our society that people need to take a stand against?

What I Think My Community Needs To Be a Better Place

A Sharing Circle

Objectives:

The students will:
— identify areas of needed improvement in their community.
— describe how they as individuals can make a difference.

Introduce the Topic:

The Sharing Circle topic for today is, "What I Think My Community Needs To Be a Better Place." How do you think your community could be improved? Perhaps you live in an area where there are a lot of people out of work, and you would like to see more done to bring businesses and employment opportunities to the area. Maybe you think that if people of different races, ethnic backgrounds, and lifestyles talked to each other more, there would be less conflict. Do you think that environmental standards need to be improved—that people need to pay more attention to picking up trash, repairing and restoring neglected buildings, and planting trees? Would you like to add more laughter and love and take away anger and hatred? Would you improve the schools, or try to get more people involved in government? Think for a bit about all the things that could be done and describe the one you think most important. Today's topic is, "What I Think My Community Needs To Be a Better Place."

Discussion Questions:

1. What would it take to actually realize the improvements we talked about?
2. What can you do to make your community a better place?
3. What could a group of young people accomplish in a community if they had a goal and were well organized?

Something I Can Do to Promote Peace and Understanding in the World

A Sharing Circle

Objectives:

The students will:
— identify ways in which they can contribute to world peace.
— describe recent world events that have promoted global peace.

Introduce the Topic:

Today in our circle, we're going to talk about peace on a broad scale. We're going to talk about global peace. Our topic is, "Something I Can Do to Promote Peace and Understanding in the World."

What can you do as a student and a citizen to make the world a more peaceful, just place? Maybe you can join an organization that works for world peace, or write letters to members of congress asking them to do more to promote equality and justice here at home. Perhaps you can send food to people in other parts of the world who are being hurt by war. Reading the newspaper so that you know what is going on in the world is a good place to start. Promoting inclusion and interdependence at home, at school, and in your neighborhood contributes to understanding and peace, too. Does your church or synagogue have activities that promote peace? Have you

ever written a letter to a member of the armed services who can't come home for the holidays? Think about it for a few moments and tell us about a way that you can make a difference. The topic is, "Something I Can Do to Promote Peace and Understanding in the World."

Discussion Questions:

1. How do you feel when you do something that helps others?
2. Why is it important to help people in other parts of the world?
3. What would it take for you to actually follow through on your ideas?

One Thing I Would Do If I Were Leader of the World for a Day

A Sharing Circle

Objectives:

The students will:
— state a priority for world change.
— describe how vision can lead to change.

Introduce the Topic:

There are many things that need to be accomplished in the world. Countries need to find ways of feeding their people and controlling population growth; young democracies need support and encouragement so that their citizens will remain free; the entire planet needs protection from things like ozone depletion, global warming, mountains of accumulated waste, and AIDS. Today, we're going to imagine what we would do if, for one day, we had the power to make any change we wished. Our topic is, "One Thing I Would Do If I Were Leader of the World for a Day."

If you became the world's leader for 24 hours and had unlimited power to make one change, what would you do? What is your vision? Perhaps you would order shelter built for all the homeless, or distribute surpluses of food to hungry people. Maybe you'd stop all fighting and violence. Or maybe you'd eliminate AIDS from the planet. Would you give every unwanted child a loving family? Would you save some species from extinction? Be imaginative! When you are ready to share, the topic is, "One Thing I Would Do If I Were Leader of the World for a Day."

Discussion Questions:

1. What feelings would you experience if you had that kind of power? What were your feelings while you were imagining?
2. What is vision, and why do we need to have it?
3. How does vision become reality? What processes are involved?
4. How important is it for individuals to link their personal vision to a broader world vision?

Additional Topics

A Time When Sharing Prevented a Fight

I Solved a Problem Effectively

A Time I Was Afraid to Face a Conflict

I Tried to Solve a Problem Too Soon

A Time Humor Saved the Day

I Faced a Problem on My Own

We Compromised to Get It Done

When the Easy Way Out Made Things Worse

How I Helped a Friend Resolve a Conflict

I Almost Got Into a Fight

I Got Blamed for Something I Didn't Do

I Got Involved in a Conflict Because Something Unfair Was
    Happening to Someone Else

A Time I Controlled Myself and the Situation Well

A Time I Was Involved in a Misunderstanding

A Time Someone Put me Down, But I Handled It Well

I Started a Conflict Between My Friends

A Way I Show Respect for Others

How I Felt When the Other Side Won

A Time I Was Misunderstood

A Time Poor Communication Caused a Fight

We Solved a Problem by Listening to Each Other

A Time I Accepted and Included Someone

A Time I Was Discriminated Against

A Way I'm Different From My Friends

I Was Rejected Because of Something I Couldn't Change

A Situation in Which I Behaved Responsibly

I Didn't Do Something Because I Knew It Would Hurt Someone

Something I Do to Protect the Environment

When a Stranger Needed Some Help

Something I've Done or Could Do to Improve Our World

I Helped Someone Who Needed and Wanted My Help

A Time When Different Opinions Led to a Conflict

We Disagreed, But We Respected Each Other's Opinion

If your heart is in Social-Emotional
Learning, visit us online.

Come see us at
www.InnerchoicePublishing.com

Our web site gives you a look at all our other Social-Emotional
Learning-based books, free activities, articles, research, and
learning and teaching strategies. Every week you'll get a new
Sharing Circle topic and lesson.

INNERCHOICE Publishing
15079 Oak Chase Court
Wellington, FL 33414

Printed in the USA
CPSIA information can be obtained
at www.ICGtesting.com
JSHW060748020823
45560JS00010B/68